Council of the Church Association

An indictment of the bishops

Shewing how the Church of England is being corrupted and betrayed by them

Council of the Church Association

An indictment of the bishops

Shewing how the Church of England is being corrupted and betrayed by them

ISBN/EAN: 9783337283483

Printed in Europe, USA, Canada, Australia, Japan

Cover: Foto ©Lupo / pixelio.de

More available books at **www.hansebooks.com**

AN INDICTMENT

OF

THE BISHOPS,

SHEWING HOW THE

Church of England is being
Corrupted and Betrayed by them

AND (INDIRECTLY) BY

The Prime Ministers:

FORMULATED BY THE
COUNCIL OF THE CHURCH ASSOCIATION.

TOGETHER WITH

Some items of interest in connection with the Conspiracy to Romanize the Church of England and some important and startling statistics showing the state of the English Dioceses.

London:
CHURCH ASSOCIATION, 14, BUCKINGHAM STREET, STRAND, W.C.
1898.

CONTENTS

	PAGE
EXTRACTS FROM PROTESTANT DIVINES	4
THE INDICTMENT SET FORTH	7
BRIEF EXPLANATION OF SIGNS, &C., USED IN THE FOLLOWING PAGES	38

UNDER EACH DIOCESE WILL BE FOUND—

> The personal Acts of the Bishop in support of the Romeward Movement.
>
> A list of Ritualistic Clergymen selected by the Bishops, past and present, for Honorary Offices, with the names of the Secret Societies to which they belong, and the Popish Practices in which they indulge.
>
> A list of "Conspirators" selected by the Bishops for promotion to Livings, with similar information.
>
> A list of Churches in which the Bishops allow Masses for the Dead to be said.

CANTERBURY, ARCHBISHOP OF	39
YORK, ARCHBISHOP OF	44
LONDON, BISHOP OF	48
WINCHESTER, BISHOP OF	51
DURHAM, BISHOP OF ...	53
BANGOR, BISHOP OF ...	54
BATH AND WELLS, BISHOP OF	55
BRISTOL, BISHOP OF ...	57
CHESTER, BISHOP OF ...	58
CHICHESTER, BISHOP OF	60
ELY, BISHOP OF	62
EXETER, BISHOP OF ...	64

	PAGE
GLOUCESTER, BISHOP OF	66
HEREFORD, BISHOP OF	69
LICHFIELD, BISHOP OF	70
LINCOLN. BISHOP OF ...	72
LLANDAFF, BISHOP OF...	75
MANCHESTER, BISHOP OF	77
NEWCASTLE, BISHOP OF ...	79
NORWICH, BISHOP OF ...	80
OXFORD, BISHOP OF ...	81
PETERBOROUGH, BISHOP OF ...	84
RIPON, BISHOP OF	85
ROCHESTER, BISHOP OF	86
SALISBURY, BISHOP OF	88
SOUTHWELL, BISHOP OF	90
ST. ALBANS, BISHOP OF	93
ST. ASAPH, BISHOP OF	96
TRURO, BISHOP OF	97
WAKEFIELD, THE BISHOP OF...	99
NATURE AND OBJECTS OF THE SOCIETIES AND PETITIONS MARKED IN THE LISTS	100
EXTRACTS FROM BOOKS publicly recommended by the Bishops to be used by Candidates for Ordination, shewing how Young Men fresh from College are crammed with Popery at the instigation of the Bishops ...	103
ITEMS OF INTEREST: The A. P. U. C., The O. C. R., The S. O., The G. A. S., The Cowley "Fathers", The "Hail, Mary", Images, Confession, Union with Rome	111
THE LINCOLN CASE	113
SOME ACTION WHICH MAY BE TAKEN BY A DIOCESAN BISHOP	115
STATISTICS SHEWING HOW THE CHURCH IS BEING ROMANIZED IN EACH DIOCESE ...	116
LIST OF BISHOPS APPOINTED BY LORD SALISBURY ...	118
,, ,, ,, ,, OTHER PRIME MINISTERS	118
STATISTICAL ABSTRACT SHEWING THE GROWTH OF ROMISH PRACTICES IN THE CHURCH OF ENGLAND	119

AN INDICTMENT

OF

THE BISHOPS.

"WHAT ARE THE BISHOPS DOING?" is a cry now heard on every hand. **The Church of England is in danger,** from Papal foes without, and **Romanizing clergy within** the fold. The hosts of Rome encamp around her on every side, aided by **thousands of clerical traitors** within; alarm and indignation widely prevail amongst her most loyal sons and daughters; and discord and disunion, instead of peace and quietness, are sown broadcast throughout the land. "Grievous wolves" have entered in amongst us, "speaking perverse things, to draw away disciples after them" (Acts xx.-29, 30). Under circumstances such as these, St. Paul's exhortation to the "overseers" of the Church of God was to "watch." But many of the Bishops of the Church of England, **instead of watching, have gone to sleep!** It is to be feared that there is only too much truth in the assertion which has been made, that the favourite petition of many Bishops is "Give peace, in *our* time, O Lord"! And meanwhile the Roman enemy without continue their attacks, and **the traitors within plot** and labour for the surrender of the fold to the men without. And the terribly sad and solemn thought is that every one of these men, without a solitary exception, has **been admitted within the fold by the Bishops** themselves, and by no other, and has by them been ordained and placed over the flock committed to his charge. The chief under-shepherds have opened the doors of the sheepfold, and have admitted, and even welcomed, the " ravening wolves" who have come to destroy the innocent sheep for whom Christ died. The Church is rent asunder, and the air is thick with coming disasters. Meanwhile not a few of the Bishops, comfortably settled in their Palaces, and enjoying all the blessings of this life, Gallio like, care for none of these weightier things, which occupy most men's minds. If ever they do wake up for a moment from their comfortable sleep of indifference, it is only **to growl at the Protestants** who are urging them do their duty, or else **to encourage,** by their smiles and patronage, the men who are working all **the mischief.** Ample proof of these charges will be found in the following pages. But though they sleep, they sleep on a volcano, like their predecessors Laud and his brother Bishops of the seventeenth century. " They are shepherds that cannot understand" (Isaiah lvi.-11).

And yet the Bishops are all, as the above quotations* from the form for the Consecration of Bishops prove, under very solemn promises, not only " to banish and drive away all erroneous and strange doctrine contrary to God's Word," but also to **" encourage others to do the same."** Alas! we have again and again to ask, when do they encourage others in this Godly work? Do they not rather discourage them to the utmost of their power? Formal complaints against false doctrine taught by clergymen have again and again been addressed to members of the Episcopal Bench, but only to be either coldly acknowledged in the most formal manner possible, or else treated with unmitigated contempt. They seem to think that they are the Church's masters, " Lords over God's heritage " (1 Peter v.-3), instead of being the Church's servants, as much subject to her rules as the humblest clergyman or layman in their dioceses.

* See Wrapper, page ii.

MODERN "MASS" IN THE CHURCH OF ENGLAND.

By the kind permission of Francis Peek, Esq.

What a contrast is this picture to the story in the Gospels of the Institution of the Supper. Here is a man pretending to "Offer" to God His own Son who is now at His right hand reigning in glory, and this under the pretence of making Him afresh to be a propiatory "offering" for sin: (Heb. x.-2). And here are other men bowing down before the Cup of which He bade them "ALL drink," but of which few, if any, of the "worshippers" intend to partake.

The Lights are burned "before the Sacrament" to shew that It is God and may be worshipped and bowed down to, as the heathen do "before their images"; while the priest stands between the people and the consecrated idol to shew that he is a "Mediator between God and man," so that "no man cometh to the Father but by the priest." "This is a deceiver and an AntiChrist."

The following pages constitute a serious "Indictment of the Episcopal Bench," yet, serious as it is, it represents **only a part of the misdeeds of the Prelates.** It is impossible to exhibit all their wrongdoing in helping on the Ritualistic cause in the Church of England; yet it will startle and surprise many loyal Churchmen to find in the following pages abundant evidence that **Episcopal sanction has been given** to many things which are a grievous offence to all true lovers of the Protestant Reformation. It is clearly proved that one or other of the Bishops* has—

1. Shielded lawless Romanizing clergy from the righteous indignation of their parishioners.
2. Vetoed the prosecution of law-breakers.
3. Consecrated churches containing illegal and Popish ornaments.
4. Taken part in, and thus practically sanctioned, services in which illegal and superstitious ceremonies were practised before his eyes.
5. Assumed the power of granting Dispensations from observing the Church's laws.
6. Granted permission to use Manuals of Devotion full of Popish doctrines.
7. Granted permission to celebrate Eucharists and to offer Prayers for the Dead.
8. Taught that the clergy of the Church of England are Sacrificing priests.
9. Endeavoured to prevent clergymen from imitating the example of the Lord Jesus in holding Evening Communion.
10. Worn the Popish Mitre, and also the Cope when not sanctioned by the law.
11. Prevented clergymen from delivering Protestant lectures.
12. Introduced the Crucifix into his private chapel.

* **One Bishop on the Bench has not made a single Ritualistic appointment of any kind so far as we can discover; and four others, who have taken no part in Ritualistic practices, have made so few that it is reasonable to suppose they have been deceived. It would not be right therefore to include them in so serious a charge as that of having "betrayed the Church of England."**

13. Given active assistance to the work of Monks and Nuns.
14. Given his patronage to Ritualistic institutions.
15. Favoured the proposed Roman Catholic University for Ireland.
16. Permitted, without public rebuke, the regular offering of Masses for the Dead in churches subject to his control.
17. Personally taught Romish doctrines by voice or pen.
18. Presented Crosses to Deaconesses.
19. Bowed to "altars" and Incense Bearers.
20. Appointed Romanizing Examining Chaplains.
21. Recommended Candidates for Holy Orders to study books teaching Popish doctrines.
22. Presented to livings in his patronage a large number of Romanizing and law-breaking clergymen.
23. Done his utmost to destroy the Protestantism of the Church of England.

The Bishops, we repeat, are not the Church, but the Church's servants, and therefore the Church has a right to call them to account for their misdeeds, and for **neglect of their solemn promises and bounden duty.**

What a startling comment on **Episcopal faithlessness** to a solemn trust the lists—given below—of clergymen promoted by them to dignities and livings afford! Instead of driving away the "grievous wolves," the Bishops have handed over the sheep of the flock to be devoured by them. In 1884, the Church Association circulated a similar list.* In the Introduction to that document occurred the following remarks, which apply equally to the present list of Episcopal Patronage:

"The following pages supply materials for a noteworthy commentary on the action of some of our Prelates, in relation to the 'strange doctrine' and 'disobedience' mentioned in their Consecration Vows. 'If a son shall ask bread of any of you that is a father, will he give him a stone?' is a question which our Blessed Saviour once asked, when here upon earth (Luke xi.-11). The Protestant parishioners of many of the parishes of which Bishops are Patrons, have asked for spiritual bread, but in a large number of cases—as is here fully *proved*—the Bishops have given them a stone. When a vacancy has occurred they have asked for

---

* *Episcopal Patronage in the Church of England.* By Walter Walsh. With a Preface by Lord Ebury. (London: W. Kent & Co. 1884.)

Protestant ministers of the Gospel, but their 'Fathers in God' have sent them Romanizing priests! Is it any wonder that such appointments have made many Churchmen sore at heart?

"The extent of Episcopal patronage conferred on the Romanizing clergy is not fully shown in the following lists. No account is therein given of Incumbents favourable to the Romeward movement who are in possession of benefices in the *alternate* gift of the Bishops, because it was found impossible to ascertain how far each Prelate has been concerned in such appointments. Had it been possible to ascertain the particulars concerning these *alternate* presentations—which are hundreds in number—the lists would, undoubtedly, have been still more enlarged. Then, with regard to the livings which are named, it is to be taken into account that the holders in many instances, by virtue of their office, have each one or more Incumbencies in their gift. No doubt these latter Incumbencies are, in the majority of cases, given to Romanizers. Are not the Bishops morally responsible for these appointments also?

"Nor is the appointment of ordinary curates foreign to our subject, though a list of those who are journeying Romeward is not supplied in this edition. The editor of *Crockford's Clerical Directory*, in his Preface to the edition of 1881, remarks—'The curate is not curate to the Incumbent, nor is the Incumbent in a position to speak of him as "*my* curate." It would be well to remind the clergy what are the real facts of the case. The Incumbent *nominates* the curate, but he does not *appoint* him, this is the Bishop's office' (p. ii). That being the case, what a fearful amount of responsibility rests on the Bishops in this matter. A careful estimate has lately been made, by the writer, of the number of curates in the Church of England who have publicly assisted the Ritualistic movement: with the result that he has by him the names of close upon two thousand such curates, every one of whom has departed from the ranks of decided Protestantism. When one contemplates the spiritual havoc wrought by the majority of these curates, their Confessionals, their Masses for the living and the dead, their idolatrous adoration of the consecrated Sacrament, their Popish ritual, and superstitious practices, we may well be anxious for the future of our Church. In view of the efforts now being made by such curates, and other clergy, to undo the work of the Reformation, there is a special cause for prayer that God 'may so guide and govern the minds' of the Bishops of our Church that, *after* as well as *before* Ordination, they may 'faithfully and wisely make choice of fit persons to serve in the sacred ministry' (Prayer for Ember Weeks).

"On the other hand it is fully admitted that in several instances much may be said in favour of the Bishops.' Like the rest of mankind they are liable to make mistakes, and, even those among them who are most loyal to the principles of the Church of England are probably deceived at times by clergymen, desirous of preferment, passing themselves off as '*moderate* Churchmen,' while in reality they are decided Romanizers. Yet even in these cases a little cross-questioning of candidates might have prevented many an unfortunate appointment. Due allowance must also be made for the fact that, as years roll on, Incumbents sometimes develop their Ritualism, and, with increased velocity, gravitate toward Rome."

The lists of Benefices given below include only those to which the present occupants were presented by Bishops who are *now alive*. Livings occupied by clergymen who were presented to them by deceased Bishops are not included in the list. Had these latter been included, the lists would have been nearly double the size. But the lists of dignities in the gift of the Bishops include appointments made by past as well as present Bishops. In order that the present occupants of the Sees may not be censured for appointments which they did not make, the year of each appointment is given. The only known directory to illegal ritual adopted in parish churches is that published by the Ritualistic English Church Union, with the title of *The Tourists' Church Guide*. This is our authority for describing the ritual of the clergymen named in these lists. It is worthy of note in this place that many clergymen who preach distinctly Romish doctrines, and are members of Ritualistic societies, have often only a very moderate ritual in their churches. On the other hand, many clergymen who have the most extreme Romanizing ritual in their churches, never allow their names to appear in the lists of Ritualistic societies, and never sign any petitions in favour of Ritualism. It is important further to note that we do not assert that all the clergymen named in our Episcopal Patronage list are in exactly the same position with regard to the Ritualistic Movement. How far they have gone away from Protestantism is indicated by the signs attached to their names, and we hold them responsible only for that which those signs signify. **Members of the E.C.U. defend Ritual because it is the expression of doctrine and because it (the Ritual) is found in practice to be the most efficient teacher of doctrine.** We assert that each clergyman named has done something which is inconsistent with the profession of Protestantism.

Full particulars of Episcopal Patronage are given in the following pages, but it may here be useful to supply the reader with a summary of statistics.

INCOMES OF EPISCOPALLY-APPOINTED INCUMBENTS, WHO HAVE SUPPORTED RITUALISM, AS DESCRIBED BELOW. PAGE 39 *et seq.*, WITH POPULATION COMMITTED TO THEIR CHARGE.

Bishop-Patrons.	No.	Value of Livings.	Population.
Canterbury	34	£12,932	244,170
York ...	44	10,686	173,387
London ...	20	5,068	113,767
Winchester	10	2,893	75,077
Durham	9	4,172	64,308
Bangor	9	1,631	11,059
Bath and Wells ...	2	535	3,094
Chester	11	2,631	13,148
Chichester	12	3,837	59,922
Ely ...	17	4,298	36,133
Exeter ...	8	1,794	13,515
Gloucester	49	10,661	169,325
Hereford ...	1	300	916
Lichfield ...	20	4,997	79,810
Lincoln ...	26	6,264	106,762
Llandaff ...	18	3,826	153,146
Manchester	15	3,957	68,545
Newcastle	1	200	16,000
Norwich ...	7	1,237	20,944
Oxford ...	45	11,102	102,189
Ripon ...	9	2,071	16,812
Salisbury ...	34	7,150	58,889
Southwell	22	5,950	106,896
St. Albans	20	5,063	101,766
St. Asaph...	9	2,862	25,482
Truro ...	9	2,239	11,725
TOTAL	461	£118,356	1,879,787

Painfully large as these figures are, they represent in reality only about 60 per cent. of the Episcopal Patronage given to those who support Ritualism.

The secret **Society of the Holy Cross*** is but a small body, and therefore it was not to be expected that many of its members would appear in the lists given below. It is a **most mischievous** as well as **secret organization**. The statistics of livings presented to members of this Society by the Bishops are as follows:

---

* The Names of the Members of the Holy Cross Society are given in *Church Association Tract, No.* 214, price 1d.

MEMBERS OF THE SECRET SOCIETY OF THE HOLY CROSS PROMOTED BY LIVING BISHOPS.

Bishop.	No.	Value of Livings.	Population.
Ely	3	£181	11,957
Gloucester	1	74	406
Lichfield	1	280	7,509
Salisbury	1	133	1,190
Southwell	2	440	16,988
St. Albans	1	293	880
Total	9	£1401	38,930

The **Confraternity of the Blessed Sacrament,*** established to promote the "Real" Presence, the **Sacrifice of the Mass, Auricular Confession,** and a host of other Romish doctrines and practices, ought to be viewed with stern displeasure by all Bishops who love the Reformation. Yet, instead of frowning on its members, several of the Bishops give them livings, and entrust hundreds of thousands of immortal souls to their care, as the following figures prove :—

MEMBERS OF THE CONFRATERNITY OF THE BLESSED SACRAMENT PROMOTED BY LIVING BISHOPS.

Bishop.	No.	Value of Livings.	Population.
Canterbury	2	£460	14,790
York	7	1,374	23,619
London	1	235	6,487
Winchester	3	560	16,957
Chichester	3	1,244	8,326
Ely	7	1,202	20,644
Exeter	1	122	2,761
Gloucester	8	1,650	40,239
Lichfield	4	1,090	21,818
Lincoln	10	2,643	21,116
Llandaff	2	309	13,400
Norwich	1	70	780
Oxford	4	999	22,464
Salisbury	7	1,496	7,291
Southwell	5	1,010	26,543
St. Albans	2	358	5,717
Truro	3	850	8,441
TOTAL	70	£15,672	261,393

* The names of 1700 Members are printed in *The Secret Work of the Ritualists*, published by the Church Association. Price, post free, 2½d.

The principal disturber of the peace of the Church of England during the past thirty years has been the **Romanizing English Church Union.** It has helped on and **encouraged** all the **Ritualistic lawbreakers** who have been prosecuted and condemned for their misdeeds, and has advocated the **Corporate Reunion** of the Church of England **with the apostate Church of Rome.** Bishops who would frown on the Church Association smile on the English Church Union, and give its members comfortable livings. One of the worst offenders in this respect is the Bishop of Gloucester who charged the Ritualists with "digging the grave of the Establishment"! The **English Church Union** has been greatly comforted and **aided by the Bishops,** in the exercise of their Episcopal Patronage, as the following statistics prove.

MEMBERS OF ENGLISH CHURCH UNION PROMOTED BY LIVING BISHOPS.

Bishop.	No.	Value of Livings.	Population.
Canterbury	10	£3,253	69,787
York	16	3,576	49,700
London	5	1,315	49,163
Winchester	4	1,130	29,691
Durham	3	971	17,691
Bangor	7	1,280	5,380
Bath and Wells	1	285	1,725
Chester	4	800	17,302
Chichester	6	1,675	32,991
Ely	11	2,734	25,714
Exeter	3	594	5,359
Gloucester	18	3,551	66,705
Hereford	1	300	916
Lichfield	7	1,860	20,159
Lincoln	16	4,083	71,959
Llandaff	6	1,167	31,682
Manchester	2	361	3,532
Newcastle	1	200	16,000
Norwich	4	702	6,862
Oxford	19	4,727	44,211
Ripon	5	930	14,697
Carried forward	149	£35,494	581,226

Bishop.	No.	Value of Livings.	Population.
Brought forward	149	£35,494	581,226
Salisbury	19	4,134	39,537
Southwell	12	2,747	65,712
St. Albans	10	2,535	59,063
St. Asaph	1	359	2,612
Truro	6	1,732	11,883
TOTAL	197	£47,001	760,033

In the appointment to the higher offices of the Church the Bishops have helped on the Ritualistic Movement to an alarming extent, as the following statistics of **dignitaries promoted by their lordships** prove. In some Cathedrals almost every Canon, Hon. Canon, or Prebendary is a High Churchman. which has now very often come to mean a Ritualist.

ARCHDEACONS WHO HAVE SUPPORTED RITUALISM, APPOINTED BY PAST AND PRESENT BISHOPS.

Diocese.	Number
York	2
Winchester	1
Durham	1
Bristol	1
Chester	1
Chichester	1
Exeter	1
Gloucester	1
Lincoln	1
Manchester	1
Norwich	1
Oxford	3
Peterborough	2
Rochester	1
Salisbury	2
Southwell	1
St. Albans	3
Truro	2
Wakefield	2
TOTAL	28

CANONS RESIDENTIARY WHO HAVE SUPPORTED RITUALISM, APPOINTED BY PAST AND PRESENT BISHOPS.

Diocese.	Number.
York	2
Durham	3
Bath and Wells	1
Chester	2
Chichester	3
Ely	2
Hereford	2
Lichfield	1
Lincoln	1
Llandaff	1
Manchester	2
Peterborough	2
Ripon	1
Salisbury	2
Truro	2
TOTAL	27

EXAMINING CHAPLAINS WHO HAVE SUPPORTED RITUALISM APPOINTED BY PAST AND PRESENT BISHOPS.

Bishop.	Number.
York	1
London	1
Durham	3
Bangor	1
Bath and Wells	2
Bristol	2
Chester	1
Ely	4
Exeter	2
Lichfield	1
Lincoln	2
Llandaff	2
Manchester	2
Newcastle	2
Norwich	1
Oxford	2
Rochester	1
Salisbury	2
Southwell	3
St. Albans	2
Truro	4
Wakefield	3
TOTAL	44

Hon. Canons and Prebendaries who have supported Ritualism appointed by past and present Bishops.

Cathedral	Number.
Canterbury Cathedral	9
York Cathedral ...	8
London, St. Paul's Cathedral ...	9
Winchester Cathedral	14
Durham Cathedral	8
Bristol Cathedral	6
Chester Cathedral ...	9
Chichester Cathedral	18
Ely Cathedral	14
Exeter Cathedral ...	10
Gloucester Cathedral	3
Hereford Cathedral	16
Lichfield ...	12
Lincoln Cathedral	29
Llandaff Cathedral ...	2
Manchester Cathedral	10
Newcastle Cathedral	13
Norwich Cathedral ...	4
Oxford Cathedral ...	16
Peterborough Cathedral	6
Ripon Cathedral ...	3
Rochester Cathedral	10
Salisbury Cathedral ..	18
Southwell Cathedral ...	15
St. Albans Cathedral	13
St. Asaph Cathedral	2
Truro Cathedral ...	19
Wakefield Cathedral	8
Wells Cathedral	15
Total.	319

We now turn to another aspect of the general subject before us. It is reasonable to assume that no Bishop would accept the office of "Visitor" of any institution until he is fully acquainted with its rules, objects, and methods of work. His acceptance of the office is rightly assumed by the public as equivalent to an Episcopal approval of the institution. It cannot for one moment be supposed that he would become "Visitor" of an institution of which he disapproved. It is, therefore, most important, in connection with an "Indictment of the Bishops," to call public attention to the assistance their lord-

"I woul
upon them as
human infirm
your name, w
you answer."-

ships give, in this way, to the work of the Romanizers in the Church of England.

To begin with the **Society of the Sacred Mission,** we learn from *The Ely Diocesan Calendar*, for 1898, p. 222, that the **Bishop of Ely is the "Visitor"** of this institution, whose headquarters are at Mildenhall, in his lordship's diocese. The Society of the Sacred Mission is, in reality, a Monastic Order, as appears by the official statement which is printed in *The Ely Diocesan Calendar*, where we read that one of the "objects" of the Mission is "to bind together in the Religious Life those [men] working for God who seem called to that state " (p. 222). It is well known that the term **" Religious Life "** for men is equivalent to the **Monastic Life.** Only those men are allowed to become members of this Monastic Order who " have determined to give *their lives*—(a) without pay or salary, (b) without marriage " (*ibid*., p. 223). From an official statement issued by the Mission we learn further: " The Life is that of a Religious House, and candidates must be willing to learn to live—(1) in restraint, and under submission to rules and to orders, by the sacrifice of self-will and personal dignity; (2) in poverty and simplicity of life." All this is, of course, equivalent to the usual Monastic Vows of Poverty, Chastity, and Obedience. In the chapel attached to the " House of the Sacred Mission," Mildenhall, advanced Romanizing ritual is used, including the use of Incense, Popish Vestments, "Altar Lights," Eastward Position, and the Mixed Chalice. **And all this under the patronage of the Bishop of Ely.** *The Kalendar of the English Church*, for 1898, p. 282, says of the Society of the Sacred Mission : " It has received formal **commendation from the Lord Bishop of Ely,** who has become its Visitor, and from whom it has received formal recognition as a Theological and Missionary College." No doubt this attempt to revive Monasticism is greatly assisted by the publication of the Bishop of Ely's name as "Visitor." Before the Mission removed from its quarters in Vassall Road, Brixton, it was* **under the patronage of the**

---

* Its Trustees, appointed by the Bishop, were Sir J. W. B. Riddell, of the E. C. U., and the Rev. C. F. Brooke, of the C.B.S. Two of its "Provincials" are also C.B.S. men.

Bishop of Rochester (Dr. Talbot), who not only acted as its "Visitor," but in other ways warmly assisted its operations. At present, says *The Official Year-Book of the Church of England,* for 1898, "the Home is **under the direction of the Bishop of Ely**" (p. 151).

Early in the year 1898 this Society of the Sacred Mission issued privately a circular to the Ritualistic clergy, in which they offered grants at a reduced rate of a new *Catechism of Faith and Practice,* printed at their own private press, for use in Sunday Schools. It is one of the most thoroughly Romish Catechisms to be met with, as the following brief extracts will prove. The italics are ours:—

"Where is our Lord Jesus Christ?

"Our Lord Jesus Christ as God is everywhere: as God *and Man* He is in Heaven *and in the Blessed Sacrament of the Altar.*

"What is Christ doing for us in Heaven and in the Blessed Sacrament of the Altar?

"Christ is offering Himself to God for us in Heaven *and in the Blessed Sacrament of the Altar*" (pp. 9, 10).

"By what means are sins forgiven?

"Sins are forgiven chiefly by Baptism *and Penance*" (p. 15).

"Where do the souls of the good go after death?

"After death the souls of the good *go to be purified from sin*" (p. 16).

"How many Sacraments are there?

"There are *seven* Sacraments: Baptism, Confirmation, the Holy Eucharist Penance, Holy Orders, Matrimony, Holy Unction" (p. 18).

"What is the Sacrament of Penance?

"Penance is the Sacrament by which sins after Baptism are forgiven" (p. 19).

"What is Confession?

"Confession is to accuse ourselves of our sins before a Priest.

"Is it a grievous sin to hide what we have done wrong in Confession?

"Yes; it is *a very grievous sin* to hide what we have done wrong in Confession: *It is to lie to the Holy Ghost*" (p. 20).

"What is Unction?

"Unction is a Sacrament in which sick people are anointed with Holy Oil" (p. 23).

"For whom must we pray?

"We must pray for all men living . . and for the souls of the faithful dead" (p. 27).

The Bishops who give their patronage to a "Mission" that teaches such unscriptural and Popish doctrines as those just quoted, cannot escape a measure of responsibility for the evil done by such teaching.

The Bishop of Chichester (Dr. Wilberforce) has recently become the "Visitor" of the **St. Margaret's, East Grinstead, Sisterhood.** The members of this Sisterhood are expected to teach young girls how to make a full confession of their sins to a priest. The Sisters take Vows of Obedience, Chastity, and Poverty, *for life*. The services in their private Oratory are of a most advanced character, and they employ a considerable portion of their time in making Romish vestments and ornaments for the use of the Ritualistic clergy. The Sisterhood publishes books full of Romish doctrines, some of them containing even Intercession of Saints. Full proofs of these charges are given in Walsh's *Secret History of the Oxford Movement*,* pages 83, 172, 173, 193, 194, 200. The thoroughly Romanizing work of this Sisterhood will, no doubt, be greatly aided by the patronage of the Bishop of Chichester.

Many other Sisterhoods have also received important aid from Episcopal patronage. Amongst others **the Bishop of London is Visitor of the St. Katherine's Sisterhood, Fulham,** of which the Rev. Alfred Gurney (a member of the Romanizing Confraternity of the Blessed Sacrament, and of the English Church Union) is Warden, and the Rev. James Longridge (a member of the secret Society of the Holy Cross) is Sub-Warden.

The Bishop of Southwell is Patron of the Belper Sisterhood, which is worked under ultra-Ritualistic guidance.

The Bovey Tracey House of Mercy, worked by the Clewer Sisterhood, **has the Bishop of Exeter as Visitor,** and the Archdeacon of Barnstaple (a member of the Confraternity of the Blessed Sacrament, and of the English Church Union) as Warden.

The St. Raphael's Convalescent Home, Torquay, is worked by the Clewer Sisterhood, and "the institution is carried on **with the sanction of the Bishop of Exeter,** who has kindly consented to act as Visitor" (*Kalendar of the English Church*, for 1898, p. 255).

---

* May be obtained from the Church Association. Price 10s 6d *net*, post free 11s.

The Bussage House of Mercy is conducted by a Sisterhood, with the **Bishop of Gloucester** as Visitor. The Chaplain is the Rev. Donald E. Robertson, a member of the Confraternity of the Blessed Sacrament, and of the English Church Union.

The Clewer Sisterhood has for its Visitor the Bishop of Oxford; and for its Warden, Canon T. T. Carter, who has been three times sheltered from prosecution by the Bishop's Veto, and was founder of the C. B. S., and one of the chief rulers of the secret Society of the Holy Cross.

The Bishop of Wakefield is Visitor of the Horbury House of Mercy, of which Canon Sharp (a member of the Confraternity of the Blessed Sacrament, and of the English Church Union) is Warden, and the Rev. J. E. Swallow, a member of the secret Society of the Holy Cross, is the Chaplain.

The Archbishop of Canterbury is Visitor of the All Saints', Margaret Street, Sisterhood, and the Rev. R. L. Page (one of the notorious Cowley Fathers) is the Chaplain.

The House of Charity, Soho, London, is worked by a special Sisterhood. **The Archbishop of Canterbury is Patron,** and **the Bishop of London is the Visitor.** Its Chaplain, the Rev. J. J. Elkington, is a member of the Confraternity of the Blessed Sacrament, and of the English Church Union.

Of **the St. Peter's Sisterhood, Kilburn, the Bishop of London is Visitor.**

The Bishop of Oxford is Visitor of the Sisterhood of St. Thomas's, Oxford, of which the Rev. A. G. Playfair (a member of the English Church Union) is the Chaplain. **His Lordship is also Visitor of the Wantage Sisterhood,** of which the Bishop of Reading is the Warden.

Amongst other institutions to which Episcopal patronage has been extended, may be mentioned the **London Diocesan Penitentiary,** of which **the Bishop of London is Visitor,** and of which the Warden is the Rev. J. H. Amps, a member of the secret Society of the Holy Cross.

The London Diocesan Deaconess Institution, of which the Bishop of London is both Visitor and President, and of which the Rev. H. P. Denison, an ultra-Ritualist, is one of the Wardens.

The St. Andrew's Mission Society was "founded" by the present Bishop of Salisbury (Dr. J. Wordsworth) in 1886, and "the staff of the Mission is under the immediate control and direction of the Bishop" (*Sarum Diocesan Kalendar*, for 1898, p. 134). There are seven "Diocesan Missioners" connected with this Society, of whom three are members of the Romanizing English Church Union (viz., the Revs. T. B. Waitt, R. de C. Thelwall. and A. E. G. Peters), and one (the Rev. R. de C. Thelwall) is also a member of the Romanizing Confraternity of the Blessed Sacrament. These gentlemen are from time to time sent out into different parts of the diocese by the Bishop, to undertake temporary duty during vacancies in livings, and to conduct Missions. It cannot be supposed that Protestants can have any confidence in the ministrations of clergymen connected with such Ritualistic societies. For all the spiritual evils, and unscriptural doctrines they may teach, the Bishop of Salisbury must be held primarily responsible.

In the Diocese of Salisbury three clergymen are appointed as "Bishop's Examiners" of Church Schools in the diocese, of whom one (the Rev. W. Gardiner) is a member of the Romanizing English Church Union, and another adopts the Eastward Position at Holy Communion. In the same diocese there are two "Bishop's Examiners of Sunday-school Teachers," one of whom (the Rev. S. Dugdale) adopts the Eastward Position, uses the Mixed Chalice, and burns "Altar Lights" in the daytime.

St. Augustine's Missionary College, Canterbury, has for its "Visitor" the Archbishop of Canterbury, who, together with the Archbishop of York and the Bishop of London, elect the Warden, Sub-Warden, and Fellows. The present Warden, who was appointed in 1880, is the Rev. G. F. Maclear, D.D., whose published writings are strongly in favour of many Ritualistic* doctrines. He is responsible for the conduct of Divine Service in the College Chapel, where the Eastward Position is adopted at Holy Communion, and "Altar Lights" are burnt in the daytime. There are three Fellows of the College, of whom one (the Rev. H. B. Cartwright) is a member of the Romanizing English Church Union, and of the Confraternity of the Blessed Sacrament.

It were much to be desired that **the Bishops** should exercise a more careful supervision, in the interests of Reformation principles, over the **Theological Colleges** for the training of the clergy of the Church of England, of which **they are Presidents or Visitors,** as the case may be. It is somewhat difficult to apportion the amount of responsibility which attaches to their lordships for what goes on within these Colleges, or to discover how far they are responsible for the selection of the College staffs. But, holding the high office of President or Visitor, they cannot altogether escape responsibility. We have already dealt with one of these Colleges, viz., St. Augustine's, Canterbury; and now we desire to call attention to others, which enjoy Episcopal patronage. The names of the officials in these Colleges are taken from *The Handbook of Theological Colleges for 1898.*

To begin with **St. Aidan's College, Birkenhead,** of which **the Bishop of Chester is Visitor.** In the services in the College Chapel the Eastward Position is adopted at Holy Communion, the Mixed Chalice is in use, and "Altar Lights" are burnt in the daytime. Its Lecturer in Pastoral Theology is the Rev. C. E. Dandridge, Vicar of Linslade, where he wears the Romish Vestments, and burns "Altar Lights" in the daytime.

The Bishop of Oxford is Visitor of Cuddesdon College, which has ever been a nursery for extreme Ritualists, several of whom have "gone over" to Rome. Its present teachers do not, so far as we are aware, belong to any Ritualistic society, yet its Principal, the Rev. J. O. Johnston, one of the editors of *The Life of Dr. Pusey,* as Vicar of Cuddesdon, adopts the Eastward Position at Holy Communion, uses the Mixed Chalice, and burns "Altar Lights" in the daytime.

* See *Church Intelligencer,* XIII., 15, 30.

The Bishop of Chichester is Visitor and President of **Chichester Theological College.** Its Principal, Canon Tenlon, is a member of the English Church Union.

The Bishop of Bath and Wells is Visitor of Wells Theological College. Its Principal, the Rev. H. P. Currie, is a member of the Confraternity of the Blessed Sacrament, and of the English Church Union.

The Bishop of Salisbury is Visitor of St. Boniface's Missionary College, Warminster. The Principal, the Rev. Sir J. E. Philipps, Bart., is a member of the Confraternity of the Blessed Sacrament.

The Bishop of Ely is Visitor of Ely Theological College. In its chapel the Eastward Position is adopted at Holy Communion. the Mixed Chalice is in use, and "Altar Lights" are burnt in the daytime. Its Principal, Canon B. W. Randolph. is a member of the English Church Union. The Vice-Principal, the Rev. F. W. Hutchinson, is a member of the English Church Union, and so also is the Chaplain, the Rev. A. H. O. M'Cheane. *The Lesser Hours of the Sarum Breviary. translated and arranged according to the Kalendar of the Church of England*, has been adopted for the **Ely Theological College.** It claims that the festival of **Corpus Christi,** in honour of the transubstantiated **wafer,** is to be observed. The book is saturated with **Mariolatry.** In a Latin Litany in this book, **precedence is given** to the **Pope,** with Bishops and "Abbots," **over the Queen.** (See *Church Intelligencer*, December, 1889, p. 180.)

The Bishop of Ripon is Visitor of the Leeds Clergy School. The Warden is the Vicar of Leeds, who, in his Parish Church, adopts the Eastward Position at Holy Communion, uses the Mixed Chalice, and burns "Altar Lights" in the daytime. The Vice-Principal. the Rev. J. B. Seaton. is a member of the English Church Union.

The Bishop of Oxford is Patron of St. Stephen's House, Oxford, which is a **Theological College.** In the chapel the Eastward Position is adopted at Holy Communion, the Mixed Chalice is in use, "Altar Lights" are burnt in the daytime, and the Romish Vestments are worn. The Principal, the Rev. C. E. Plumb, is a member of the Confraternity of the Blessed Sacrament, and of the English Church Union.

The **Bishop of Oxford is Visitor of Dorchester Missionary College.** Its Vice-Principal, the Rev. R. U. Potts, is a member of the English Church Union.

In addition to the above the following Theological Colleges, in High Church hands, are **under Episcopal patronage,** viz.: **Lichfield Theological College; Salisbury Theological College; Scholæ Cancellarii, Lincoln; Truro School of Divinity;** and **Burgh Missionary College.**

It will, no doubt, surprise many readers to learn that such a large number of Theological Colleges for training the future clergy are in High Church or Ritualistic hands. The grave nature of this evil cannot easily be over-estimated. If the wells are poisoned, how shall the people have pure water? It is most important that Protestant parents who intend their sons to become clergymen should be careful not, on any account, to send them to Theological Colleges, where the teaching staff are more or less Ritualistic. Happily there are Theological Colleges where the students are taught on Reformation lines, such as St. John's Hall, Highbury; Wycliffe Hall, Oxford; and Ridley Hall, Cambridge. These valuable and important institutions are worthy of the increased support of Evangelical Churchmen.

In the choice of an **Examining Chaplain, each Bishop has a free hand.** Unhappily many members of the Episcopal Bench have selected for this high and most important office clergymen who are zealous partisans of the sacerdotal party, and members of extreme societies of a Romanizing character. The names of these Examining Chaplains will be found in the following pages. The late Archdeacon Denison, when Examining Chaplain to a former Bishop of Bath and Wells, refused to pass for Ordination any young man who did not profess his faith in Baptismal Regeneration and the Real Presence. Subsequently he gloried in acting thus. (See his *Notes of My Life*.)

Is there not grave reason to fear that other Examining Chaplains of the Ritualistic party act in the same way? We do not assert that it is so in every instance: yet there can be little doubt that the possibility that it might be so in their own case has kept many an Evangelical young man from offering himself for Ordination in a diocese under Ritualistic control. No member of any society teaching Romish doctrines ought to be allowed to hold the influential office of Examining Chaplain. Loyal Churchmen have a just cause for alarm and dissatisfaction with the Bishops on this subject. We do not wonder that during the past few years the number of candidates for Holy Orders has decreased largely. The prospect of having to pass through the hands of Ritualistic Examining Chaplains has, no doubt, a great deal to do with this decrease.

In connection with the subject of **Ordination, the Bishops are guilty** of **a serious misuse of the powers** entrusted to them, by recommending for the study of candidates for Holy Orders a large number of **books which teach Popish doctrines.** In the following pages a selection only has been made from these books, and extracts from them are given, with full references in each case, proving that, under Episcopal guidance, advice, and recommendation, the future clergy are, in certain English dioceses, expected to study works teaching—

1. Purgatory.
2. Intercession of Saints.
3. Seven Sacraments.
4. Extreme Unction.
5. Transubstantiation and the Real Presence.
6. The Eucharistic Sacrifice for the Living and the Dead.
7. Reunion with the apostate Church of Rome.
8. Reunion with the corrupt Eastern Church.
9. Auricular Confession.
10. Prayers for the Dead.
11. That the English Protestant Martyrs were mostly "fanatics."
12. The praise of the Oxford Movement.
13. The alleged benefits of Convents.
14. Priests as necessary mediators between Laymen and God.

Is it to be wondered at that so many of our English clergy are Romanizers, when **the Bishops** thus **recommend Popish doctrines** for their acceptance, and that at the most critical time in their youth, before their theological opinions are finally fixed ? To recommend such Romanizing books to them, under such circumstances, is almost, if not quite, equivalent to *forcing* Popery into the minds of the future clergy of the Reformed Church of England.

As we have already stated, we do not in these pages give an account of all **the misdeeds of the Prelates** in helping on **the Romeward Movement,** and undoing, so far as possible, the work of the Reformation. There is **much which is done privately** in this direction. Private Episcopal influence, private Episcopal conversation, go a long way with many of the clergy. Not a few of the more timid Protestants are prevented from coming out boldly on the Protestant side, through fear of what their Bishops may say or do. The fear, in only too many instances, is not groundless. The hands of the High Church Bishops are often heavy on the Protestant clergy, in ways the public never hear about. **The present Archbishop of York,** when Bishop of Lichfield, refused to allow a Church Association vicar to have a much-needed curate, solely because of the vicar's decidedly Protestant views. In multitudes of rectories and vicarages throughout the land painful and sore feelings against the Bishops are smothered up because it would not be safe to give expression to them. . The whole world knows how powerful is the influence, and how **zealous are the efforts,** which certain **Bishops have made** in trying **to force the Evangelical** and law-abiding clergy **to give up Evening Communion,** and **to adopt the surplice** in the pulpit instead of the preaching gown, declared legal by the courts of law. And yet these Evangelical clergy, often sorely harassed and persecuted by the Bishops, are the men who, more than any others, are first in rendering due obedience to the laws of the Church, and are zealous in good works. The Bishops, however, will learn, it may be sooner than they at present think, that the party which has, under God, produced the Church Missionary Society, the Church Pastoral Aid Society,

THE CRUCIFIX AT ST. PAUL'S.

The above represents the Reredos at St. Paul's Cathedral. It will be observed that in the centre is a Crucifix, and elevated high above the Image (in Sixt [...] Second Commandment) is another Image of the Virgin Mary, so idolatrously adored by Roman [...] and revered as "Queen of Heaven." According to the Church of Rome, the Crucifix is a part of the Ritual [...] part of Mass; yet when the citizens of London wished to test the lawfulness of this erection, which [...] were prepared to show had received idolatrous veneration, Bishop Temple and Archbishop of Canterbury stopped the proceedings.

and a host of other organizations for the glory of God and the spiritual and bodily welfare of mankind, is too strong to be safely despised, ignored, or persecuted. The Evangelicals, more than any others, represent the views of the Protestant Reformers. They existed in the Church long before Ritualists were heard of, and they do not intend to be driven out now. It may be that the English Nation will again, as in the seventeenth century, though with less violent methods, learn the great lesson taught by the "Judicious Hooker," in the extract from his works given above, namely, that it is not by any "heavenly law" but "by force of custom" that the Bishops rule, and that it is within the power of the Church to take the authority which the Bishops now possess from them. The learned Bishop Jewel's words will find an echo in many hearts in this nineteenth century: "Some say, the Bishops be they that should redress the Church. Would to God they would!" But, with Jewel, we have only too much reason to fear that they will do nothing of the kind. The remedy of the present great evils, schisms, and contentions in the Church of England is apparently, not to be sought for on the Episcopal Bench, but, under God, rests with the people of England. The *laity* must reform the Church themselves.

We complain often enough, and not without reason, that **Prime Ministers appoint** High Church and **Ritualistic,** instead of decidedly Protestant **Bishops.** But, after all, here comes in the question, With whom does the fault *primarily* rest? Is it not with the people of England themselves? If the electors voted as they ought, only for Protestant Members of Parliament, no Government would be allowed to exist which, through the Prime Minister, nominated unfaithful and Ritualistic Bishops. Meanwhile, and until a more effectual remedy can be applied, public opinion can do much to cripple Episcopal powers for mischief. We can demand **the abolition of the Episcopal Veto,** so powerful in shielding the Ritualistic law-breakers from the just consequences of their misdeeds. Loyal Churchmen can **refuse to subscribe** even the smallest sum **to Diocesan Societies** whose funds go to centralize patronage and, more or less, to support the work of the Pope in the Church of England. Why should Protestants give money to pull down their own house in which they live? **The Romanizing Bishops must be made to fear the Protestantism of England,** when they refuse to be moved by higher considerations. The Council of the Church Association in presenting to the public this "Indictment of the Bishops," **desire to emphasise the gravity of the evils** to which they here direct attention, and to point out that, unless an efficient remedy is immediately applied, there is every reason to fear that the evil will increase as the years go on. **The Bishops** have sinned by omission as well as commission; they have, with a few exceptions, inexcusably **neglected their duties;** and, apparently, have **forgotten their consecration vows** to "banish and drive away all erroneous and strange doctrine contrary to God's Word." Here, if anywhere, they ought to be "not slothful in business" (Rom. xii. 11). But, alas! it must be said, that "By much slothfulness the building decayeth; and through idleness of the hands the house droppeth through" (Eccles. x. 18). Their sins of commission are set forth in this "Indictment." Nothing seems to delight **certain Bishops** more than to be seen in vestments which make them **look like genuine Popish prelates.** They have **made friends with the enemies of the Protestant Reformation,** and frowned upon its best friends. They have heaped honours on those who have turned their backs on the good old ways of our forefathers. They have appointed **28** supporters of Ritualism as **Archdeacons;** and **27** to Residentiary **Canonries,** with handsome salaries attached to each of them. The enormous number of **319** supporters of Ritualism have received **Hon. Canonries from the Bishops.** Their lordships have presented at least **70** members of the **Romanizing Confraternity of the Blessed Sacrament** to livings in their gift, and have given them **£15,672 every year** to do their work among 261,393 immortal souls. **197** members of the Romanizing and lawless **English Church Union** have received **livings from the Bishops,** with no less than **£47,001** a year to labour for **the destruction of Protestantism** among 760,033 souls. But this by no means exhausts their sins of commission. **Supporters of Ritualism** are now receiving as the gifts of **unfaithful Bishops,** the gigantic sum of **£118,565 a year** every penny of which ought, on the principles of common justice, to have been given only to men who maintain the Protestant faith pure and undefiled. **Their lordships** have handed over **a vast population** of not less than **1,879,787 persons** to the care of men, not one of whom, had they lived at the beginning of this century, would have received any favour from the Episcopal Bench.

The Council of the Church Association appeal to the Protestants of England, and ask them to do their duty in this weighty matter. **Unless the Bishops do their duty they ought to be turned out of office,** and faithful men placed in their room. We have had, of late, too much of proud Prelates; we want humble bishops who will faithfully take care of the flocks committed to their charge, men who will love the sheep more than the wolves, and who, like the Martyr Bishops of the Sixteenth Century, will be willing rather to die, than allow Popery to have its way in the Church of England. Let every faithful Protestant offer daily the prayer of the dying King Edward VI.:

"O Lord God, save Thy chosen people of England! O my "Lord God, defend this Realm from Papistry, and maintain "Thy true religion, that I and my people may praise Thy Holy "Name, for Thy Son Jesus Christ's sake."

BRIEF EXPLANATION OF SIGNS, &c.,
Used in the following pages.

+ . . Member of the Society of the Holy Cross.
C. . . Member of the Confraternity of the Blessed Sacrament.
U. . . Member of the English Church Union.
L. . . Signed Petition for Licensed Confessors.
N. . . Signed Confraternity of the Blessed Sacrament Declaration in favour of Non-Communicant Attendance at Holy Communion, *i.e.*, "Hearing Mass."
D. . . Signed Declaration of the Three Deans in favour of the Eastward Position and Vestments.
V. . . Signed Petition to Convocation in favour of the Popish Vestments.
T. . . Signed Petition of 1881 for the Toleration of Extreme Ritual.
P. . . Signed Remonstrance against the Purchas Judgment.
i. . . Incense.
v. . . Popish Vestments, such as the Chasuble, Albe, Stole, &c.
al. . . "Altar Lights" burnt in the daylight.
ep. . . Eastward Position at Holy Communion.
mc. . Mixed Chalice.

MASSES FOR THE DEAD.

V. . . Vespers for the Dead.
S. . . Sermon advocating Prayers and Masses for the Dead.
HE. . "Holy Eucharist for the Dead."
L. . . Litany for the Dead.

For the **Nature and Objects of the Societies** referred to, see p. 100.

N.B.—It must be clearly understood that—
1. It has been found impossible to indicate the presentations to Benefices in the "alternate" gift of the present Bishops.
2. The appointments to Benefices by deceased Prelates are not given, the list would be nearly doubled if they were.
3. That the Ritualistic Clergy appointed by the Bishops have frequently other churches in their gift, and that all the Curates of these Incumbents are selected by them.

The Treacherous Acts of the Bishops
AND HOW THEY HAVE
Broken their Consecration Vows,
THUS RENDERING THEMSELVES
Liable to be Impeached by Parliament.

The Archbishop of Canterbury, Dr. Temple.

Salary, £15,000 a year and a Palace.

Consecrated 1869. Translated in 1897, by **LORD SALISBURY.**

When Bishop of Exeter.
(1) He promises to protect the Lawless Clergy from the Law Courts.

(a) "I am prepared to bind myself to be governed by the decision of the Archbishop on appeal if any clergyman presented for ritual or doctrine were to submit himself to *me*. I should in that case stop all proceedings against him on the ground that he had obeyed the Prayer Book by referring the question to the Bishop [!], and I should then hear him personally, and after consideration, should announce the decision I was prepared to give . . if, in the exercise of my discretion, I thought it better to make no order, either as regards the whole matter in dispute, or as regards certain particulars in it, *I should be bound by no decision at all.*"—*Charge*, 1884.

(b) "If it could be said that the Bishops had no power to protect the clergy *from the Courts* it might be said that the Bishops should come in as judges; but when the Bishops had the power to begin with, he did not see how they could call on the State to grant them any more."—*Speech in Convocation*, July, 1884.

When Bishop of London.
(1) He consecrates Churches full of Popery.

(a) Consecrated St. Cuthbert's, Philbeach Gardens, and took part in a high celebration, himself celebrating, with lights, sanctus bell, and crucifix; and at a later celebration, on the same day, there were no communicants with the priest. The Bishop's attention being called to this, he did nothing whatever. —*Church Intelligencer*, V.-3 and 17.

(b) Consecrated "Church of the Holy Redeemer," Clerkenwell, with a crucifix over the altar, stations of the cross hung on the walls, six vesper lights burning, and a space set apart in body of church as a confessional.—*English Churchman*, 1888, p. 656.

(c) Consecrated St. Anselm's, Davies Street, W., containing seven sanctuary lamps, six candlesticks on main "altar," and on south side of the edifice a second "altar." Also took part in a procession through stable-yards, &c., a pastoral staff being carried before.—*Protestant Observer*, 1896, p. 41.

(2) He takes part in, or sanctions by his presence, disloyal practices condemned by the Queen's Courts.

(a) He preached at St. Columba's, Haggerston, October 5th, 1896, and took part in a procession headed by a cross and two lighted candles, he being censed by the Rev. D. Cameron.—*English Churchman*, 1896, p. 666.

(3) He treats the complaints of distressed Churchmen with contempt.

(a) Repeated complaints of extreme ritual at St. Ethelburga, Bishopsgate, by the churchwardens. No acknowledgment of these complaints, and no alteration made in the church, or service.—*English Churchman*, 1888, p. 745.

(b) Attention being drawn to a tabernacle, images of Virgin and of our Lord with a "sacred" ace-of-hearts, crucifixes, and sacring bells, at St. Clement's, City Road, the complaint was merely acknowledged.—*Protestant Observer*, 1893, p. 151.

(c) When complaint was made of an image of Virgin with candles before it, at St. Michael's, Shoreditch, Dr. Temple took no action.—*Rock*, 1897, p. 703.

(4) He grants Dispensations from imaginary obligations.

(a) He dispensed the clergy and congregation of All Saints', Margaret Street, from the obligation to keep All Saints' Day, November 1st (a Friday) as a fast day, in order to keep the parochial festival of their church.—*English Churchman*, 1889, p. 710.

(b) He granted a dispensation from vows to Rev. F. P. Downman, who had been seeking to found an order of men and had failed, after nine years' trial. Vows taken September 8th, 1875.—*Rock*, 1889, December 27th, p. 5.

(c) He released a clergyman in the East End of London from the vow of celibacy.—*English Churchman*, 1890, January 17th, p. 10.

(d) At a public luncheon in connection with St. Alban's, Holborn, vicar stated that a dispensation from fasting had been obtained from Bishop of London.—*Rock*, 1895, July 5th, p. 3.

(5) He sanctions that which he ought not.

(a) The Rev. T. Lacey, in *Church Times*, March 25th, 1898, says the Bishop "authorised" the use of the Manual of the C. B. S. with the exception of one Litany. The special Litany not being specified we take the following extracts from various parts of the Manual:—

This Manual teaches the Romish doctrine of the "turning" of the bread into the Body (p. 91); Adoration of the host (pp. 32, 50, 65); Concomitance (p. 39 ; "Intention" (p. 18); "Hearing mass" (pp. 6, 67); "Veiled" presence "contained" "under" forms, on altars, and in hands (pp. 31, 44, 45, 91); a perpetual Offering of Christ as a "Victim" in heaven on an altar there (pp. 53, 69); and also as a "Victim" on the "altars" on earth (pp. 46, 47, 59, cf 19, 21).

(b) The Bishop of Argyle performed Popish rites at the dedication of a

Memorial chapel at St. Alban's, Holborn, *with the sanction of the Bishop of London.*—*Rock*, 1892, March 11th, p. 7.

(c) Sanctioned a crucifix, erected by Sir Edward Clarke, &c., at St. Peter's, Staines.—*Rock*, 1894, August 31st, p. 5.

(d) The Rev. Morris Fuller states in *Church Times*, December 17th, 1897, that Bp. Temple gave him permission in writing to place a crucifix on the side of the chancel arch, and to use the Stations of the Cross, Compline, Tenebrae, and three hours' service: though the Chancellor of the Diocese afterwards ordered the removal of the " Stations " pictures as being " superstitious."

(6) He introduces a new Service into the Church of England.

(a) He read a "sentence of Reconciliation" at St. Paul's Cathedral, on the occasion of an "act of reparation to Almighty God for the dishonour to His sanctuary." A protest against this was sent by Captain Cobham, which was merely acknowledged.—*Rock*, 1890, November 7th. p. 5.

(7) He permits Romish Requiem Masses.

(a) After the Bishop of London's attention had been called to a requiem mass at St. Alban's, Holborn, for the soul of Mr. Mackonochie, he promised to "inquire into the matter." Yet on December 15th, 1891, he allowed Bp. Chinnery-Haldane to celebrate mass for the same purpose in the same church, *without communicants*, but with elevation, crucifix, torches, sacring bells, &c. (*Church Intelligencer*, V.-21, IX.-6). *The Church Review*, in reporting this, states that Bp. Haldane officiated by the "express permission" of the Bishop of London.

(b) Gave permission to the Rector of Old St. Pancras to have a special annual celebration of the Holy Eucharist to commemorate the dead (see also *Rock*, December 8th, 1893, p. 5, and *Protestant Observer*, 1894, pp. 16 and 20).—*English Churchman*, 1893, p. 826.

(c) *The Guardian* of December, 1893, reported that written permission had been given by Bp. Temple for using a collect, epistle and gospel not authorised by the Prayer Book and to celebrate Holy Communion as a "Commemoration of the faithful dead," with illegal vestments and garbled service. The Bishop refused to take any action.

When Archbishop of Canterbury.

(1) He takes part in illegal services.

(a) Archbishop Temple took part in Service of Holy Communion at St. Paul's Cathedral, during which four "altar" lights were burning.—*Rock*, 1897, p. 369.

(b) At St. Paul's (August, 1897) wore for the first time a Pectoral cross.—*English Churchman*, 1897, p. 873.

(2) He does that which brings discredit upon his high office.

(a) In addressing a letter to "certain ecclesiastical dignitaries in Russia," he dates it, as "on the Day of the Annunciation of the most holy Mother of God, and ever Virgin Mary."—*Rock*, 1897, p. 408.

(b) Held it no "ecclesiastical offence" to exhibit holy bones alleged to be those of St. Eanswythe at Folkestone.—*English Churchman*, 1897, p. 873.

(3) In his reply to the Pope's Bull he claimed—

That clergy of the Church of England are sacrificing priests in the same sense as are those of the Church of Rome. And that the Lord's Supper is a sacrificial offering in the same sense as the Jewish burnt-offerings.

RITUALISTIC APPOINTMENTS BY PAST AND PRESENT ARCHBISHOPS.

Date of Preferment.	Name.			Ritualistic Societies and Petitions.		Ritual.
	HON. CANONS.					
1863	H. Bailey	...	...	D.T.P.		
1872	H. A. Jeffreys	...	...	D.T.P.		
1888	W. Benham	...	...	U.T.P.	...	ep., v., al.
1888	J. W. Bliss	...	...	C.U.V.T.P.	...	ep., al.
1890	F. H. Murray	...	...	C.U.L.N.D.V.P.	...	ep., mc., v., al.
1893	R. S. Hunt	...	...	U.D.V.T.P.	...	ep., al.
1893	M. Woodward	...	...	C.U.V.P.	...	ep., mc., al.
1895	A. Whitehead	...	...	U.T.P.		
1896	F. E. Carter	...	...	T.		
	SIX PREACHERS.					
1885	J. Cullin	...	...	...	...	ep., al.
1893	A. H. Lang	...	...	C.U.		
1895	F. E. Carter	...	...	T.		
1896	A. W. Robinson	...	...	...	...	ep., mc., al.
	CHAPLAIN.					
1883	Dean of Rochester	...	...	C.U.L.N.V.T.P.		

ARCHBISHOP TEMPLE'S APPOINTMENTS TO BENEFICES.

Living.	Incumbent.	Date of Appt.	Yearly Value £	Population.	Ritualistic Societies and Petitions.‡	Ritual ‡
*Bethnal Green, St. John	E. R. Hollings	1892	242	12,000	U.T.	ep., v., al.
*Bow, St. Mary	M. Hare	1892	320	7,010	...	ep.
*Ealing, Christ Ch.	W. T. King	1895	500	6,000	v.	ep., mc., v., al.
*Ealing, St. Peter	W. Petty	1894	500	3,100	...	ep., mc., v., al.
*Fulham, St. And.	E. S. Hilliard	1891	300	20,000	T.	ep.
'Fulham, St. Clem.	W. P. Hindley	1886	280	7,000	...	ep., mc., al.
*Fulham, S. Dionis	J. S. Sinclair	1886	400	10,000	...	ep.
*Shepherd's Bush, St. Luke	W. St. H. Bourne	1887	530	10,000	...	ep.
*Shepherd's Bush St. Stephen	E. G. Wood	1893	200	10,000	v.	ep., al.
*Highgate, St. Mic.	W. R. Ogle	1895	500	4,000	...	ep., mc.
*Hillingdon, S. Jn.	C. M. Harvey	1895	503	2,644	...	ep., mc., al.
*Hillingdon, S. And.	H. G. Bird	1891	300	2,688	v.	ep., mc., v., al.
*Pentonville, S. Sil.	R. Leach	1887	325	9,833	...	ep.
*Notting Hill, S. Cl.	C. E. T. Roberts	1886	300	10,874	...	ep., mc., al.
*Notting Hill, St. James, Norlds.	R. S. Hassard	1893	550	9,914	...	ep. mc., al.
*Earl's Court, St. Matthias	son	1892	300	5,602	C.U.D.V.	ep.,i.,mc.,v.,al.
*Knowle, St. Giles	F. W. Hatham	1893	114	85	...	ep.
*Limehouse, S. Jn.	J. H. Haden	1893	294	5,241	...	ep., mc., al.
*Mile End New Town, All Sts.	J. B. Rust	1891	290	6,000	T.	ep.
*Nuthurst	G. K. Boyd	1892	161	811	...	ep., mc., v., al.
*Paddington, All St.	W. Boyd	1893	600	5,811	...	ep., al.

APPOINTMENTS TO BENEFICES—continued.

Living.	Incumbent.	Date of Appt.	Yearly Value £	Population.	Ritualistic Societies and Petitions.	Ritual.
*Kensal Green, St. John	R. Thornber ...	1891	400	22,000	... ...	ep.
*Isle of Dogs, S. Jn.	D. G. Cowan ...	1892	216	6,050	v. ...	ep., r., al.
*London, Christ Ch., Watney St.	H. C. Dimsdale	1892	160	9,188	c.v. ...	ep., r , al.
*London, All Sts., Margaret St. ...	W. A. Whitworth	1886	381	2,641	v. ...	ep., r., al.
*London, Christ Ch., Albany St.	F. T. Hetling...	1890	374	11,025	v d.v.t.p.	ep., al.
*Haggerston, S. Pl.	H.W. Goodheart	1890	350	7,603	... ...	ep., mc., al.
*Stepney, St. Mat.	G. J. H. Llewellyn ...	1894	230	6,200	..	ep.
*Stoke Newington, St. Andrew ...	F. Belton ...	1895	1,000	7,169	... ...	ep.
†Teignton Regis...	P. Jackson ...	1878	337	1,707	t. ...	ep.
*Noel Park, St. Mk.	R. B. Dowling	1890	278	7,500	t. ...	ep.
*Twickenham, H. Trinity	P. B. Drabble	1891	580	4,593	v.	ep.
†Ufficulme	H. Bramley ...	1875	197	1,806	d.v.	
*London, St. Anne, Soho	J. H. Cardwell	1891	920	8,075	v.t. ...	ep., mc., al.
Total			£12932	244,170		

* While Bishop of London.   † While Bishop of Exeter.

MASSES FOR THE DEAD.

The Archbishop allows Requiem Masses for the dead, under the Guild of All Souls, to be publicly celebrated in the following Churches in his Diocese:—

The Annunciation, Chislehurst. v., he.   St. Michael's, Croydon. he.
St. Nicholas's, Chislehurst. v., he.   St. James's, Elmley. he.
St. Barnabas's, Margate. s., he.   St. Paul's, Ramsgate. he.
St. Bartholomew's, Dover. v., he.   SS. Peter and Paul, Headcorn. he.
St. Mary's, Canterbury. v., he.   St. Saviour's, Folkestone. he.

Archbishop of York, Dr. Maclagan.

Salary, £10,000 and a Palace.

Consecrated 1878. Translated 1891 by LORD SALISBURY.

When Bishop of Lichfield.
(1) **Uses his influence to stop Evening Communion.**

(a) Required of clergymen, before their preferment, that they would not introduce Evening Communion, or if in use, discontinue it.—*Times'* Leader, January 23rd, 1893; *English Churchman*, 1894, p. 541.

When Archbishop of York.
(1) **Takes part in illegal Romish Services.**

(a) Took part in a procession headed by a "crucifer" and attendant "acolytes," &c. Vicar walked in front of Archbishop carrying crucifix. Whilst the Archbishop preached the sermon the vicar stood before him holding the crucifix. Praised the service afterwards.—*English Churchman*, 1892, p. 661.

(b) Visits St. Columba, Middlesbrough. The service used being taken from the *Priest's Prayer Book*. Procession headed by a crucifix and banners. "Altar" vested in white with six lights burning. Sarum Ritual used.—*English Churchman*, 1893, p. 331.

(2) **Sanctions High Mass in Greek Church.**

(a) Attended High Mass on Sunday at the Russian Embassy Chapel, in Welbeck Street.—*Rock*, 1897, p. 447.

(3) **Sets his face against Evening Communion.**

(a) In his charge discouraged Evening Communion.—*English Churchman*, 1894, p. 46.

(4) **Sanctions Prayers for the Dead.**

(a) Asked the prayers of two "synods" for their brethren (named) who had died during the last twelve months.—*Rock*, 1894, July 13th, p. 3.

(5) **Selects a Romanizer for promotion.**

(a) Promoted the curate of Christ Church, Doncaster, at which Madonna and Child, two confessionals and holy water were in use. *English Churchman*, 1894, p. 715.

(6) **Snubs complaining Churchmen and does nothing to help them.**

(a) In 1895, when appealed to by the parishioners of Christ Church, Doncaster, refused to order the removal of holy water stoups, confessional boxes, a statuette of the Virgin and crucifix, introduced without any faculty.—*Church Intelligencer*, XII.-74. The image of the Virgin and a tabernacle for the reserved water were simply removed to another part of the same church (103).

The Church Times, in its leader of January 10th, 1896, says: He has "put himself forward as the champion of the Catholic faith and discipline against Protestant prejudice."

(b) *Hensall cum Heck.* On October 20th, 1896, representation made as to image of Joseph, Mary, and Crucifix, with collecting boxes for " offerings for 'Mary,' and for 'Joseph,'" with confessionals, silver hearts, &c. On March 19th, 1897, the Archbishop replied that " he was not unaware of the state of things in the parish of Hensall cum Heck, but must decline to be put in motion" by non-parishioners.—*Church Intelligencer,* XIII -149 ; XV., XIV.- 36, 52.

(c) Notice of stations of the cross, masses and confessions openly announced and purgatory preached. Collection taken to defray the expense of a black cope, at St. Silas's, Hull. " Unable" to take action.—*English Churchman,* 1897, p. 764.

(7) **Urges that clergy are " Sacrificing Priests."**
(a) In an address to the " Pastoral Order " of the Holy Ghost, tells members they are the Priests of God, and that as priesthood implies sacrifice, so sacrifice connotes an " Altar."—*Rock,* 1896, p. 19.

(8) **Issues a revised Confirmation Service without authority.**
(a) In *Diocesan Magazine* for February, 1896, desired clergy to procure and use a revised Confirmation service edited by himself from Egbert's Pontifical. —*Rock,* 1896, p. 250.

(9) **In his reply to the Pope's Bull he claimed—**
(a) That clergy of the Church of England are sacrificing priests in the same sense as are those of the Church of Rome. And that the Lord's Supper is a sacrificial offering in the same sense as the Jewish burnt offerings.

RITUALISTIC APPOINTMENTS BY PAST AND PRESENT ARCHBISHOPS.

Date of Prefer- ment.	Name.	Ritualistic Societies and Petitions.	Ritual.
	ARCHDEACONS.		
1897	W. H. Hutchings	C.U.N V.T.P.	*ep., mc., r, al.*
1892	J. Palmes	D.V T.P.	
	CANONS RESIDENTIARY.		
1894	H. Temple	D.T.P.	*ep., al.*
1896	J. Watson	T.	
	HON. CANONS.		
1876	J. Scott	V.T.P.	*ep., mc., al.*
1891	J. C. Atkinson	U.	
1895	J. Watson	T.	
1894	H. Temple	D.T.P.	*ep., al.*
1895	W. H. Hutchings	C.U.N.V.T.P.	*ep., mc., v., al.*
1895	H. E. Maddock		*ep.*
1896	C. C. Mackarness		*ep., e., al.*
1896	J. R. Keble		*ep.*
	EXAMINING CHAPLAINS.		
1891	H. E. Maddock		*ep.*
	CHAPLAINS.		
1891	Marquis of Normanby	T.P.	
1891	E. de V. Bryans	U.V.T.P.	
1891	J. R. Keble	T.	

ARCHBISHOP MACLAGAN'S APPOINTMENTS TO BENEFICES.

Living.	Incumbent.	Date of Appt.	Yearly Value. £	Population.	Ritualistic Societies and Petitions.	Ritual.
*Adbaston	T. L. Butler	1887	271	539	T.P.	ep.
Bishopthorpe	J. R. Keble	1891	246	511	...	ep., mc.
Cawood	B. E. Wake	1895	253	1,008	T.	
*Colwich	O. Dobree	1890	336	944	C.D.V.	ep.
*Coseley, Christ Ch.	W. Spencer	1883	300	8,854	V.V.T.	ep., mc., r., al.
*Coseley, St. Chad	G. C. De Renzi	1885	215	4,198	V.	ep., mc., al.
Darrington	H. S. Atkinson	1892	293	815	...	ep.
Eastwood	G. A. England	1895	340	7,500	T.	ep., mc.
*Eccleshall	W. Allen	1882	222	2,703	...	ep., al.
*Edingale	W. G. Garland	1883	114	223	V.V.T.	ep., mc., r., al.
Egton	R. G. Glennie	1895	290	905	...	ep., mc., al.
Foster-on-the-Wolds	F. Kennedy	1895	150	583	...	ep.
Fridaythorpe	A. Bathe	1894	154	280	C.U L.D.V.T.	ep., mc., i., r., al.
*Goldenhill	G. R. Bailey	1890	312	3,860	U.D.V.T.	ep., mc., al.
*Lichfield, Ch. Ch.	C. T. Abraham	1889	241	1,311	r.	ep., al.
Middlesborough, St. Paul	T. E. Lindsay	1893	211	25,571	...	ep., mc.
Newington	W. Ward	1893	300	25,000	...	ep.
*Newport, Salop	W. T. Burges	1886	233	2,764	D.P.	
*Penn	C. H. Cole-Webb	1883	310	1,196	...	ep., mc., al.
Royston	R. J. Thorp	1892	325	4,000	V.T.	
Hull, St. Silas	W. H. Baker	1894	234	5,270	...	ep., mc., i., r., al.
*Shrewsbury, St. Mary	N. Poyntz	1888	215	1,000	...	ep., r., al.
*Shrewsbury, AllSt.	P. A. E. Emson	1889	210	4,000	C.V.	ep., mc., r., al.
*Shrewsbury, H.Cr.	W. H. Draper	1889	247	2,800	...	ep., al.
*Shrewsbury, H.Tr.	C. T. Holmes	1888	200	4,500	...	ep., al.
*Tatenhill	T. Roper	1884	525	258	V.T.P.	ep.
Thirkleby	W. H. Higgins	1894	186	210	T.	
*Tividale, St.Mich.	G. R.W. Griffith	1889	245	5,000	C.V.T.	ep., r., al.
Sowerby	E. de V. Bryans	1897	230	1,876	V.V.T.P.	ep., mc.
Ugthorpe	C. Johnson	1892	173	749	...	ep.
Upleatham	J. A. Armitage	1894	286	287	T.P.	
Wales	G. L. M. Rees	1894	300	2,255	V.T.	ep., mc.
*Walsall, St. And.	R. R. W. Griffith	1889	202	7,200	C.V.	ep., mc., r., al.
*Wednesbury, St. Bartholomew	J. Eckersley	1881	247	6,962	...	ep.
*Weeford	F. C. Beaumont	1879	320	250	T.	
*West Bromwich, St. John	N. T. Langley	1888	220	8,200	...	ep., mc., al.
*Whittington	W. H. Kay	1883	254	2,009	C.U.P.	
Whitwood	H. W. Holden	1894	110	1,130	C.U.L.D.V.P.	ep., mc.
*Wolverhampton, Christ Church	A. H. Smith	1889	200	5,273	r.	ep., mc., r., al.
*Wolverhampton, St. Andrew	J. M. J. Fletcher	1885	160	5,761	...	ep., al.
*Wolverhampton, St. Mary	C. Dunkley	1882	300	8,071	T.	ep.
Yarm	V. G. Daltry	1896	169	1,485	r.	ep., mc., al.
York, HolyTrinity, Micklegate	J. Solloway	1895	138	2,076	...	ep.
York, St. Olave	W.W.Dodsworth	1892	199	4,000	C.V.	ep., mc., r., al.
TOTAL			£10686	173,387		

* While Bishop of Lichfield.

MASSES FOR THE DEAD.

The Archbishop allows Requiem Masses for the dead under the Guild of All Souls, to be publicly celebrated in the following Churches in his Diocese :—

St. Aidan's, Scarboro'. v.s., he.
All Saints', Middlesboro'. v.s., he.
All Saints', Scarboro'. v., he.
Christ Church, Doncaster. v.s., he.

St. Matthew's, Sheffield. v.s., he.
St. Oswald's, Newton-in-Cleveland. s., he.
St. Silas', Hull. v.s., he.
St. Wilfred's, Cantley. he.

Also a Requiem celebration for deceased members of the E. C. U. at St. Mary's, Sculcoates.

Bishop of London, Dr. Creighton.

Salary, £10,000 a year and a Palace.

Consecrated 1891. Translated 1897 by LORD SALISBURY.

When Bishop of Peterborough.

(1) Wears illegal Vestments.

(a) Wore a cope of white satin, and an elegant mitre of figured-satin at an Ordination. Used pastoral staff for rapping upon the portals of the church " and thus exorcised all evil spirits from the interior for ever."—*English Churchman*, 1891, p. 555; see also *Protestant Observer*, 1891, p. 130.

(b) At an ordination. Marched in procession from the Palace to the Cathedral, wearing mitre and cope.—*English Churchman*, 1892, p. 922.

(2) Revises the Communion Office without authority.

(a) Used at St. Matthew's, Northampton, a revised Communion Office with interpolated collects, prayers for dead, altered rubrics, and other Romeward alterations, St. Matthew's Day, 1893.—*Church Intelligencer*, XI.-3.

(3) Sanctions the Confessional.

(a) The Rev. J. Longridge heard confessions at Little Bowden Church with the license of the Bishop.—*English Churchman*, 1897, p. 154.

When Bishop of London.

(1) Wears illegal Vestments.

(a) Wore "mitre" and cope at Confirmation at St. Augustine's, Kilburn.—*English Churchman*, 1897, p. 167.

(b) Wore the "mitre" and cope at St. Etheldreda's, Fulham, six candles being alight.—*English Churchman*, 1897, p. 221.

(c) Confirmation at All Saints', Margaret Street, W. Wore "mitre," cope with picture of Madonna and Child on the back. Violet cassock, pectoral cross. Pronounced the Benediction with pastoral staff in his hand (April, 1897).—*English Churchman*, 1897, p. 238.

(2) Sanctions Crucifix in Private Chapel, &c.

(a) Introduced crucifix, cross, and reredos at Fulham Palace.

(b) Visited St. Mary's, Somers Town, for the purpose of "opening" a reredos containing "as large and speaking a representation of the Crucifixion of our Lord as was possible."—*English Churchman*, 1897, p. 867.

(3) Takes part in Romanizing Practices.

(a) St. Peter's, Fulham. Six vesper lights, crucifix, and second procession with priest in cope and biretta, preceded by a thurifer and two acolytes with lighted candles. The Bishop is censed. Notice of time of hearing Confessions given out in the hearing of Bishop. Recession, cross, &c.—*English Churchman*, 1897, p. 254.

(4) Welcomes the "Cowley Fathers."

(a) "Willingly" gives his consent to the proposal of the "Cowley Fathers" to have a house in London.—*English Churchman*, 1897, p. 787.

(5) The following shows what is done with the Bishop of London's Fund.

(a) Out of £20,374 raised for this Fund in one year, £11,939 was given to churches in which the following Romish practices were in use: incense, the eastward position, vestments, the mixed chalice, and altar lights, whilst m ny of the clergy are members of the Romanizing E. C. U. and C. B. S.

(6) Authorises a purely Popish Service.

(*a*) On Wednesday evening (Vigil of Corpus Christi), the " Vespers of the Blessed Sacrament" were sung (by permission of the Bishop of London). See *Church Review*, June 9th, 1898.

(7) Corpus Christi.

(*a*) The Feast of Corpus Christi, a Roman Catholic Festival, was celebrated in June, 1898, in a large number of London Churches.

RITUALISTIC APPOINTMENTS BY PAST AND PRESENT BISHOPS.

Date of Preferment.	Name.	Ritualistic Societies and Petitions.	Ritual.
	PREBENDARIES.		
1878	A. Wilson	D.V.T.P.	ep.
1880	W. Baker	V.T.	
1881	H. W. Tucker.	D.V.T.P.	
1883	G. H. Hodson	D.T.P.	ep., mc.
1887	A. Barff	C.D.T.P.	ep., mc., v., al.
1890	J. H. Snowden	T.	ep.
1896	H. M. Villiers	C.V.P.	ep., v., al.
1896	R. D. Ram		ep., mc., al.
1897	B. Compton	V.P.	
	PRECENTOR.		
1886	Canon H. Scott-Holland	C.V.	
	EXAMINING CHAPLAIN.		
1897	Hon. A. T. Lyttelton		ep., mc.

BISHOP CREIGHTON'S APPOINTMENTS TO BENEFICES.

Living.	Incumbent.	Date of Appt.	Yearly Value. £	Population.	Ritualistic Societies.	Ritual.
*Belgrave,St.Peter	R. D. L. Clarke	1892	235	6,487	C.V.	ep., mc., al.
*Belgrave, St.Mich.	W. S. Law	1895	200	8,000		ep., mc., al.
*Empingham	T. W. Owen	1892	80	110		ep., mc.
*Eye	H. J. Sibthorpe	1895	350	1,237		ep., mc., al.
*Humberstone, St. Barnabas	G. Tandy	1893	198	10,000	V.	ep., me., al.
*Knighton,St.John	C. P. Eden	1893	400	4,790	V.	ep., al.
*Leicester,St. Geo.	H. E. Sherlock	1895	301	5,900		ep., mc., r., al.
*Leicester, St. Luke	W.O.Leadbitter	1894	300	6,596		ep., mc., al.
*Leicester, St.Mart.	S. J.W. Sanders	1893	100	1,862		ep., mc.
*Leicester, St. Mary	J. Mountain	1895	306	7,150	T.	
*Leicester,St.Matt.	M. T. K. Brown	1893	361	11,000		ep., al.
*Leicester, St.Peter	W. P. Holmes	1893	350	26,000	C.T.	ep., mc., al.
*Loughborough, H. Trinity	W. Fraser	1892	302	3,976	V.T.	
*Northampton, St. James	W. P. Hurrell	1892	132	4,159		ep.
*Northampton, St. Mary	C. E. Newman	1895	153	3,000		ep., al.

APPOINTMENTS TO BENEFICES—continued.

Living.	Incumbent.	Date of Appt.	Yearly Value. £	Population.	Ritualistic Societies.	Ritual.
*Paston ...	F. W. Robinson	1893	400	810	V.T.P.	ep., me.,
*Peterborough	B. deM.Egerton	1894	272	8,000	T.	ep.
*Quorn ...	E. F. Kelcey...	1892	132	1,886	U.	ep., v., al.
*Towcester	W. H. Deane...	1895	300	2,775	...	ep.
*Wardley...	C.J.R. Berkeley	1893	196	29	T.	ep., al.
	TOTAL ...		£5,068	113,767		

* While Bishop of Peterborough.

MASSES FOR THE DEAD.

The Bishop allows Requiem Masses for the dead, under the Guild of All Souls, to be publicly celebrated in the following Churches in his Diocese :—

All Saints', Margaret Street. v., s., HE.
All Saints', Notting Hill. v., HE.
St. Augustine's, Highgate. v., s., HE.
St. Augustine's, Stepney. v., s., HE.
Berkeley Chapel, Mayfair. v., HE.
St. Clement's, City Road. v., s., HE.
Holy Cross in St. Pancras. v., s., HE.
St. Cuthbert's, Kensington. v., s., HE.
St. Ethelburga's, Bishopsgate. v., s., HE.
St. Faith's, Stoke Newington. v., s., HE.
St. Gabriel's, Bound's Green. v., s., HE.
St. John Baptist's, Kensington. v., s., HE.
St. John Baptist's, Pimlico Road. v.
St. Mary's, Charing Cross Road. v., s., HE.
St. Mary's, Edmonton. v., HE.
St. Mary Magdalene, Munster Square. v., HE.

St. Mary Magdalene, Paddington. v., HE.
St. Matthew's, Westminster. v., HE.
All Souls', Harlesden. v., s, HE.
St. Augustine's, Haggerstone. v., s., HE.
St. Matthias's, Earl's Court. v., s., HE.
Royal Small Arms Factory Church, Enfield Lock. v., s., HE.
St. Saviour's, Pimlico. v., HE.
St. Thomas's, Stamford Hill. v., s., HE.
St. Alban's, Holborn. HE.
St. Barnabas's, Pimlico. HE.
St. Bartholomew's, Bethnal Green. HE.
St. Gabriel's, Bromley. HE.
St. Mary's, Graham St., Pimlico. HE.
St. Michael and All Angels', Chiswick. HE.
St. Peter's, Ealing. HE.

Also a Requiem celebration for deceased members of E. C. U. at
St. Mary Magdalene, Paddington. | St. Barnabas's, Acton.
St. Mary, Primrose Hill.

Bishop of Winchester, Dr. Davidson.

Salary. £6500 a year and a Palace.

Consecrated 1890. Translated 1895 by LORD SALISBURY.

When Bishop of Rochester.
(1) Complainants get no redress.

(a) The Bishop was notified in 1891 that one of his clergy had published a book entitled *The sinless conception of the Mother of God*, speaking with contempt of the Thirty-nine Articles, describing the Virgin as "Co-Redemptrix" and "the only bridge of God to men," and the Pope as "the father of the faithful," whose Encyclical is reproduced as being authoritative and true. The Bishop did nothing whatever.—*Church Intelligencer*, VIII.-101.

(b) The same clergyman had been delated to the previous Bishop of Rochester for advocating in the Roman Catholic *Westminster and Lambeth Gazette* seven sacraments and the decrees of the synod of Bethlehem which sanction image-worship, transubstantiation, purgatory, the canonicity of the Apocrypha, as well as the special Intercession of the Virgin Mary. Nothing was done by the Bishop.—*Church Intelligencer*, VI.-133.

(c) Notice of Ritualistic practices, altar lights, eastward position, &c., at St. Catharine's, Hatcham. No action taken.—*Rock*, 1892, September 2nd, p. 11.

(d) Attention drawn to extreme Ritualism at St. Alphege, Southwark. "Stations of the Cross," "Prayers for the Dead," "Hail Mary," &c. No action taken.—*English Churchman*, 1893, p. 254.

(2) Presents crosses to Deaconesses.

(a) Admitted five ladies to the new office of deaconess. "Altar" draped in white. Seated himself before the "altar," candidates kneel before him, and to each he gave a *cross*, and formally ordained them by imposition.—*English Churchman*, 1892, p. 154.

When Bishop of Winchester.
(1) Joins in Romish practices.

(a) Held a confirmation in St. Agatha's, Landport. Joined in procession preceded by two acolytes carrying lighted tapers, six lights on "High Altar."—*English Churchman*, 1897, p. 221.

RITUALISTIC APPOINTMENTS BY PAST AND PRESENT BISHOPS.

Date of Preferment.	Name.	Ritualistic Societies and Petitions.	Ritual.
	ARCHDEACON.		
1888	Archdeacon of Surrey (J. H. Sapte)		ep., mc., al.
	HON. CANONS.		
1873	J. Compton		ep., mc., r , al.
1876	J. E. Clarke		ep.
1881	V. Musgrave	T.	ep., mc., al.
1882	Hon. A. Brodrick ...	...	ep.
1887	W. E. Heygate ...	V.T.P.	ep., al.

RITUALISTIC APPOINTMENTS—continued.

Date of Preferment.	Name.	Ritualistic Societies and Petitions.	Ritual.
HON. CANONS—continued.			
1889	A. C. Blunt	v.t.p.	
1889	W. H. Lucas	c.	
1889	R. J. Dundas	d.t.	ep., al.
1889	F. E. Utterton	t.	ep., al.
1890	A. Poole	v.p.	
1891	G. O. Balleine	...	ep., al.
1894	F. P. Phillips	t.	
1896	W. Durst	n.t.p.	ep., mc., al.
1897	A. G. Hunter	c.v.t.	ep., al.

BISHOP DAVIDSON'S APPOINTMENTS TO BENEFICES.

Living.	Incumbent.	Date of Appt.	Yearly Value. £	Population.	Ritualistic Societies and Petitions.	Ritual.
*Battersea, St. Ph.	E. H. Jones	1892	270	14,000	c.	ep., mc., al.
*Camberwell, St. George	R. Appleton	1894	240	16,000		ep.
*Kingston Vale, St. John	F. S. Colman	1892	230	500		ep., mc.
*Walworth, St Pt.	J. W. Horsley	1894	250	14,035	c.t.l.v.p.	ep., r., al.
*Wandsworth, St. Anne	N. Campbell	1894	271	10,235		ep.
*Wimbledon, All Saints	A. M. Pickering	1892	230	4,300		ep., mc., al.
Winchester, Holy Trinity	A. Gunn	1897	200	2,316	c.	ep., mc., i., r., al.
*Woolwich, S. My.	C. E. Estcreet	1892	592	12,035		ep., mc.
Meonstoke	A. H. Ashwell	1897	500	1,050	c.	
East Boldre	J. Caley	1897	110	606	c.c.	
TOTAL			£2893	75,077		

* While Bishop of Rochester.

MASSES FOR THE DEAD.

The Bishop allows Requiem Masses for the dead, under the Guild of All Souls, to be publicly celebrated in the following Churches in his Diocese:—

St. Agatha's, Landport.   v., s., he.
St. Alban's, Ventnor.   v., s., he.
St. Michael's, Southsea   v., s., he.
St. Nicholas's, Guildford.   v., he.
St. Peter's, Winchester.   v., s., he.

Holy Trinity, Bramley.   he.
St. Stephen's, Bournemouth.   he.
St. Michael's, Lyndhurst.   he.
Puttenham Church, Guildford.   he.

Also a Requiem celebration for deceased members of E. C. U. at
St. Michael's, Southampton. | St. Peter's, Bournemouth.
St. Mark's, Jersey.

Bishop of Durham, Dr. Westcott.

Salary, £7000 a year.

Consecrated 1890. Appointed by LORD SALISBURY.

RITUALISTIC APPOINTMENTS BY PAST AND PRESENT BISHOPS.

Date of Preferment.	Name.	Ritualistic Societies and Petitions.	Ritual.
	ARCHDEACON.		
1882	H. W. Watkins	r.	
	CANONS RESIDENTIARY.		
1880	H. W. Watkins	r.	
1883	G. Body	c.v.p.	
1889	H. Kynaston	c.v.	
	HON. CANONS.		
1867	H. Holden	v.r.p.	
1880	F. Brown		ep.
1889	J. Baily		ep., al.
1895	H. E. Savage		ep., mc., al.
1896	H. J. Richmond	r.	
1896	G. H. Ross-Lewin	r.	ep.
1896	H. C. Lipscomb	v.r.	
1897	J. T. Fowler	r.v.r.p.	
	EXAMINING CHAPLAINS.		
1890	H. W. Watkins	r.	
1890	R. Appleton		ep.
1890	H. E. Savage		ep., mc., al.

BISHOP WESTCOTT'S APPOINTMENTS TO BENEFICES.

Living.	Incumbent.	Date of Appt.	Yearly Value. £	Population.	Ritualistic Societies and Petitions.	Ritual.
Gateshead, H. Trin.	J. W. Parish	1891	277	8,147	r.	ep., mc., al.
Hartlepool, Ch. Ch.	W. F. Cosgrave	1891	314	10,277		ep., mc., al.
Hartlepool, St. Paul	E. Sykes	1894	250	8,435		ep.
Houghton-le-Spring	A. M. Norman	1895	1,400	5,622		ep.
Lumley	H. W. Stewart	1891	294	2,482	v.r.	ep., mc., al.
Ryton-on-Tyne	J. Baily	1891	607	3,283		ep., al.
Pallion, St. Luke	S. Pater	1895	300	10,000		ep., mc., al.
Millfield, St. Mark	A. R. Stogdon	1894	330	9,000		ep.
Sunderland, St. Thomas	R. T. Talbot	1893	400	7,062	r.	ep., mc., al.
Total			£ 4172	64,308		

MASSES FOR THE DEAD.

The Bishop allows Requiem Masses for the dead, under the Guild of All Souls, to be publicly celebrated at the following Church in his Diocese:—

St. Patrick's, Lintz Green. v., he.

Bishop of Bangor, Dr. Lloyd.

Salary, £4200 a year.

Consecrated 1890. Appointed by LORD SALISBURY.

RITUALISTIC APPOINTMENTS BY PAST AND PRESENT BISHOPS.

Date of Preferment.	Name.	Ritualistic Societies and Petitions.	Ritual.
	DEAN.		
1884	Very Rev. E. Lewis	T.P.	ep.
	EXAMINING CHAPLAIN.		
1890	D. W. Thomas	U.T.	

BISHOP LLOYD'S APPOINTMENTS TO BENEFICES.

Living.	Incumbent.	Date of Appt.	Yearly Value. £	Population.	Ritualistic Societies, and Petitions.	Ritual.
Bettws-Garmon	R. A. Williams	1891	233	124	r.	
Bettws-y-Coed	R. Jones	1892	120	740	...	ep.
Caerhun	J. W. Roberts	1893	180	899	r.	
Llanfacthlu	R. H. Williams	1891	302	381	r.	
Llanfair-juxta-Harlech	R. Jones	1893	119	400	r.	
Llanfair-Pwll-Gwyngyll	D. Herbert	1895	171	961	r.	
Llanidloes	E. O. Jones	1891	231	4,939	...	ep., al.
Pentraeth	E. P. Howell	1895	103	1,000	r.	
Trawsfynydd	E. B. Thomas	1892	172	1,615	r.	ep.
TOTAL			£1,631	11,059		

Bishop of Bath and Wells, Dr. Kennion.

Salary, £5000 a year.

Consecrated 1882. Translated 1894 by LORD ROSEBERY.

(1) Approves Kilburn Sisters. See "Truth."
   (a) Welcomed Kilburn Sisters into diocese.—*English Churchman*, 1894, p. 471.

(2) Sanctions Romish Practices and Prayers for the Dead.
   (a) Celebrated Mass at Frome Selwood, which has long been notorious for its advanced ritual and costly Romish vestments.—*English Churchman*, 1894, p. 855.
   (b) Took the leading part in the dedication of a memorial cross in East Brent Churchyard. This cross is surmounted by a huge representation of the Crucifixion, and contains a number of images of Popish saints, and of Archbishop Benson and Archdeacon Denison.—*Protestant Observer*, 1896, p. 27.
   (c) Confirmation at All Saints', Clevedon. Prayers for Dead, &c. Crucifix over pulpit. Procession preceded by acolyte in red and white, bearing large cross, with several banners, clergy wearing birettas. The vicar attired in crimson and gold. Then an acolyte bearing a cushion, on which lay a "mitre." Bishop with pastoral staff came last. Incense used.—*English Churchman*, 1897, p. 280.

RITUALISTIC APPOINTMENTS BY PAST AND PRESENT BISHOPS.

Date of Preferment.	Name.	Ritualistic Societies and Petitions.	Ritual.
	SUB-DEAN.		
1861	C. M. Church ...	D.P.	
	CANON RESIDENTIARY.		
1879	C. M. Church ...	D.P.	
	PREBENDARIES.		
1855	C. M. Church ...	D.P.	
1867	A. W. Grafton...	D.T.P.	
1871	J. Earle ...	T.	
1880	E. C. S. Gibson	T. ..	ep., mc., al.
1882	J. W. Robinson	D.P.	
1883	W. Michell ...	D.T.P.	
1884	G. D. W. Ommanney...	V.T.P.	
1887	E. Burbridge ...	T.P.	
1890	W. W. Herringham ..	D.V.T.P. ..	ep., mc.
1891	G. Tugwell	C.U.V.P. ...	ep., mc., v., al.,i.
1893	W. Hook ...	U.D.T.P.	
1894	J. R. Vernon ...	V.P.	ep., al.
1895	T. S. Holmes ...	T. ...	ep., v., al.
1896	H. P. Denison ...	C.N.V.	
1896	H. P. Currie ...	C.U.	
	EXAMINING CHAPLAINS.		
1894	E. C. S. Gibson	T. ...	ep., mc., al.
1897	T. S. Holmes	T. ...	ep., v., al.
	CHAPLAIN.		
1897	H. P. Currie ...	C.U.	

BISHOP KENNION'S APPOINTMENTS TO BENEFICES.

Living	Incumbent.	Date of A¡ pt.	Yearly Value. £	Population.	Ritualistic Societies and Petitions.	Ritual.
Cannington	G. A. Mahon...	1896	250	1,369	D.T.	*ep., mc.*
Pill	E. M. Lance ...	1896	285	1,725	U.	*ep., mc., c., al.*
TOTAL			£ 535	3,094		

MASSES FOR THE DEAD.

The Bishop allows Requiem Masses for the dead, under the Guild of All Souls, to be publicly celebrated in the following Churches in his Diocese :—

All Saints', Weston-super-Mare. s., HE.
St. George's, Dunster. s., HE.
St. John Baptist's, Bathwick. v., HE.
St. John Baptist's, Frome, Selwood. v., HE.

St. John Evangelist's, Highbridge. HE.
St. Katharine's, Woodlands, Frome. HE.
Holy Trinity, Taunton. HE.

Also a Requiem celebration for deceased members of E C.U. at

St. John, South Clevedon. | Holy Trinity, Taunton.

Bishop of Bristol, Dr. Browne.

Salary, £3000 a year.

Consecrated 1895. Translated 1897, by LORD SALISBURY.

When Bishop of Stepney.
(1) Takes part in Romish Practices.
(a) Expressed earnest sympathy with the work which was being carried on at St. Peter's, London Docks, where 3126 confessions had been heard and requiem masses offered.—*English Churchman*, 1895, p. 457.

When Bishop of Bristol.
(1) Again takes part in Romish Practices.
(a) Dr. Browne, when Bishop of Stepney, gave a stirring address on "St. George" at St. James', Hampstead Road, when banners of St. George, the "blessed sacrament," *i.e.*, wafer, the "Sacred Heart," "Our Lady," and a crucifix were carried in procession with lights, incense, and a hymn "appropriate to the cult of St. George was sung."—*Church Review*, April 22nd, 1897.

RITUALISTIC APPOINTMENTS BY PAST AND PRESENT BISHOPS.

Date of Prefer-ment.	Name.	Ritualistic Societies and Petitions.	Ritual.
	ARCHDEACON.		
1892	H. Robeson	D.V.T.P.	
	HON. CANONS.		
1881	H. N. Ellacombe	T.P.	
1882	J. Rich ...	E.D.T.P.	
1887	F. J. Buckley ...	E.D.V.T.P.	
1890	M. J. G. Ponsonby ...	C.V.T. ...	ep., al.
1890	C. E. Cornish ...	... ...	ep., mc., al.
1891	Dean Randall ...	C.V.T.P. ...	ep., mc., al.
	EXAMINING CHAPLAINS.		
1897	C. E. Cornish ...	...	ep., mc., al.
1897	H Robeson ...	D.V.T.P.	

MASSES FOR THE DEAD.

The Bishop allows Requiem Masses for the dead, under the Guild of All Souls, to be publicly celebrated in the following Churches in his Diocese:—

Frampton Cotterell Church. HE. | Holy Nativity, Knowle H.E.
St. Simon's, Bristol. HE. |

Also a Requiem celebration for deceased members of E.C.U. at

Holy Nativity, Knowle. | St. Katherine's, Knowle.
Frampton Cotterell Church.

Bishop of Chester, Dr. Jayne.

Salary. £4200 a year.

Consecrated 1889. Appointed by LORD SALISBURY.

(1) Defends lawbreakers.

(*a*) His first act when Bishop Designate was to attend a partisan meeting convened by Archdeacon Denison to denounce any appeal to law in matters of ritual.—*Church Intelligencer*, December, 1888.

(2) Sanctions Prayers for the Dead.

(*a*) In his charge, after reading over the names of those of the clergy who had passed away during the year, added, "May they have rest, peace and light." Also took part in a procession headed by a huge cross, vested in cope and mitre, his pastoral staff borne before him.—*Rock*, 1892, January 8th, p. 4.

(3) Takes part in Popish Practices.

(*a*) Celebrated Holy Communion in Chester Cathedral with lighted candles and adopted Eastward Position, wearing large jewelled pectoral cross.—*English Churchman*, 1894, p. 632.

(4) Disallows Evening Communion.

(*a*) Upon appointment of the Rev. W. G. Bridges to St. George's, Hyde, Cheshire, the congregation expressed a desire that he would introduce an Evening Communion. He did so, but the Bishop hearing of it, wrote informing him that he would not allow Evening Communion in any church where it had not already been in use.—*Local Correspondent*, December 17th, 1897.

(5) Disregards Protestant Complaints.

(*a*) On the Churchwardens and Parishioners complaining of illegal practices and discontinuance of Evening Communion at St. John's, Dukinfield, the Bishop replied, that he had asked the Vicar for explanations, and finds no ground for further intervention. No redress has been obtained.

RITUALISTIC APPOINTMENTS BY PAST AND PRESENT BISHOPS.

Date of Preferment.	Name.	Ritualistic Societies and Petitions.	Ritual.
	ARCHDEACON.		
1886	E. Barber	C.U.V.T.P....	*ep., mc., v., al.*
	RESIDENTIARY CANONS.		
1886	E. Barber	C.U.V.T.P....	*ep., mc., v., al.*
1886	A. J. Blencowe...	... ...	*ep., al.*
	HON. CANONS.		
1871	T. E. Espin	... ...	*ep., mc., al.*
1882	J. H. Cooper	U.D.V.T.P....	*ep., al.*
1888	A. H. Webb	.. ...	*ep.*
1889	E. J. Bell	U.... ..	
1890	A. M. Wood		*ep.*
1891	J. R. C. Miller	D.V.	*ep., mc., al.*
1892	H. A. Hignett	V.T.P. ...	
1895	P. H. Moore	V.T.P.	*ep.*
1896	S. C. Cooper	V....	*ep.*

RITUALISTIC APPOINTMENTS—continued.

Date of Preferment.	Name.	Ritualistic Societies and Petitions.	Ritual.
	EXAMINING CHAPLAIN.		
1895	A. M. Wood		ep.
	CHAPLAIN.		
1889	F. J. Wood	C.D.V.P.	ep., mc., al.

BISHOP JAYNE'S APPOINTMENTS TO BENEFICES.

Living.	Incumbent.	Date of Appt.	Yearly Value. £	Population.	Ritualistic Societies and Petitions.	Ritual.
Brighton, New ...	C. H. H. Stewart	1889	330	10,000	v.	ep.
Chester, Christ Ch.	J. F. Howson .	1889	190	5,537	... ...	ep., al.
Chester, S. Michael	A. Radford ...	1893	251	758	... ...	ep., al.
Crewe, S. Barnabas	W. C. Martin .	1891	250	4,445	... ...	ep.
Hoylake, H. Trinity	F. Sanders ...	1891	332	3,803	... ...	ep.
Flowery Field ...	T. M. Tozer ..	1894	192	4,729	v. ...	ep., mc., al.
Northwich	G. R. Sanders .	1894	150	2,000	v. ...	
Norton, Durham .	T. E. Scott ...	1890	450	4,000	... ...	ep.
Stockport, S. Augus.	A. J. Jameson .	1895	90	4,500	... ...	ep., mc., v., al.
Wallasey	W.H.L.Cogswell	1895	268	2,803	... ...	ep.
Waverton	G. J. Baillie-Hamilton ...	1892	128	573	v.	ep., v., al.
Total ...			£2,631	43,148		

MASSES FOR THE DEAD.

The Bishop allows Requiem Masses for the dead, under the Guild of All Souls, to be publicly celebrated in the following Churches in his Diocese:—

St. Martin's, Low Marple. v., s., he. | St. Mary's, High Legh. he.

Also a Requiem celebration for deceased members of E.C.U. at

St. Paul's, Tranmere. | St. James', Latchford.
St. Mark's, New Ferry. | Coppenhall Parish Church.

Bishop of Chichester, Dr. Wilberforce.

Salary. £4200 a year.

Consecrated 1882. Translated 1895 by LORD SALISBURY.

(1) Plays at Popery.

(*a*) Present at "Mass" in Memorial Church at Brighton. Roman missal followed, with Elevation and thirty-six candles. Preached and communicated.—*English Churchman*, 1896, p. 794.

(2) Objects to Evening Communion.

(*a*) Soon after translation to Chichester, publicly objected to Evening Communion being celebrated in his diocese, saying that whoever celebrated thus would incur his "severe displeasure."—*Rock*.

(3) Approves Prayers for the Dead.

(*a*) At a Diocesan Conference held in 1896 at Brighton, recommended "Prayers for the Dead."—*Hastings and St. Leonard's Observer*.

(4) No redress for Parishioners.

(*a*) BRIGHTON.—At Church of Annunciation, image of Virgin Mary outside chancel gates, lights burning before it with flowers. Complaint being made October 29th, 1896, Bishop did nothing.

(*b*) At St. Bartholomew's, complaint December 8th, 1896, from four hundred parishioners. The Mass, vestments, auricular confession, prayers for the dead, station of cross, crucifixes. Bishop said, January 26th, 1897, he had "taken order," but no alteration was made in service.

(*c*) A further complaint, March 3rd, of high mass, sung mass, prayers for dead, auricular confession. No reply and no redress. Two of the curates "went over" to Rome.

March 24th, 1896; complaint resented as being an "interference in the government of the diocese."

(5) Grants Dispensation.

(*a*) Early in 1897, granted a dispensation from fasting to the congregation of Christ Church. St. Leonard's, on the occasion of the Dedication Festival. Complaint made by several members of the congregation, but no reply vouchsafed.

RITUALISTIC APPOINTMENTS BY PAST AND PRESENT BISHOPS.

Date of Preferment.	Name.	Ritualistic Societies and Petitions.	Ritual.
ARCHDEACON.			
1888	R. Sutton	V.T.P.	*ep.*
CANONS RESIDENTIARY.			
1888	J. S. Teulon	U V.T.P.	
1889	R. E. Sanderson	V D.V.P.	*cp., mc., al.*
1896	A. M. Deane	D.P.	

RITUALISTIC APPOINTMENTS—continued.

Date of Prefer- ment.	Name.	Ritualistic Societies and Petitions.	Ritual.
	PREBENDARIES.		
1866	R. Sutton	V.T.P.	ep.
1877	W. Awdry	D.T.	
1879	J. S. Teulon	U.V.T.P.	
1882	R. E. Sanderson	V.D.V.P.	ep., mc., al.
1887	J. J. Hannah	...	ep.
1888	J. S. Barron	D.T.P.	ep., mc.
1888	P. Webb	P.D.V.T.P	
1891	H. D Jones	U.T P.	ep., al.
1891	T. Peacey	V. ...	ep., al.
1892	J. H. Simpson	U.D.V.P.	ep., al.
1894	G. W. Pennethorne	...	ep.
1896	E. Miller	D.P.	
1896	A. H. S. Barwell	D.V.T.	ep., al.
1896	J. J. Mallaby	...	ep.
1897	A. M. Deane	D.P.	
1897	H. B. Foyster	...	ep.
1897	A. B. Simpson	U. ...	ep., mc., al.
1897	J. T. Bramston	T.P.	

BISHOP WILBERFORCE'S APPOINTMENTS TO BENEFICES.

Living.	Incumbent.	Date of Appt.	Yearly Value. £	Popu- lation.	Ritualistic Societies and Petitions.	Ritual.
Bolney	T. A. Holcroft	1896	300	800	V T.	ep., mc., al.
*Cramlington	G. T. Shettle	1894	242	5,500	...	ep., mc., v, al.
*Framlington	C. B. Carr	1891	200	413	U.	ep., mc., al.
*Newcastle-on-Tne	E. J. Gough	1894	498	3,726	C.U.T ...	ep. mc., al.
*Newcastle-on-Tne St. Augustine	G. Miles	1893	200	9,300	...	ep., v., al.
*Newcastle-on-Tne St. Luke	R. Raggett	1892	60	4,000	U. ...	ep., v., al.
*Newcastle-on-Tne St. Peter	J. Wilkinson	1891	300	4,306	...	ep., al.
*Benwell, St. Jas.	H. O. Hall	1894	350	14,252	U.	ep., mc.
*Tynemouth, St. Augustine	W. L. Cunning- ham	1893	260	600	C.U.V.T.P.	ep., al.
*Wallsend, St. Pet.	J. Henderson	1886	634	3,025	... ...	ep., al.
*Wallsend, St. Lke.	W. M. O'Brady Jones	1892	307	10,000	U.	ep., v., al.
*Woodhorn	O. Rhodes	1893	486	4,000	C.	ep., mc., v. al.
TOTAL			£3,837	59,922		

* While Bishop of Newcastle.

MASSES FOR THE DEAD.

The Bishop allows Requiem Masses for the dead, under the Guild of All Souls, to be publicly celebrated in the following Churches in his Diocese:—

St. Anne's, Eastbourne. V., HE.
The Annunciation, Brighton. V., S., HE.
St. Bartholomew's, Brighton. V., S., HE.
Ch.Ch., St. Leonard's-on-Sea. V., S., HE.
St. George's, Brede. V., S., HE.
St. Martin's, Brighton. V., S., HE.

St. Mary and Mary Magdalene Brighton. V., HE.
All Souls'. Hastings. HE.
St. Andrew's, Worthing. HE.
St. Peter and Paul, Rustington, Wor- thing. HE.

Bishop of Ely, Dr. Compton.

Salary. £5500 a year.

Consecrated 1886. Appointed by LORD SALISBURY.

(1) Takes part in Romish Practices.

(*a*) At ordination in Cathedral was attired in cope. Wore mitre in procession from palace to entrance. A silver crozier was carried before him by his chaplain. Permitted each of his assisting chaplains to elevate the consecrated elements.—*English Churchman*, 1888, p. 354.

(2) Attacks Evening Communion.

(*a*) At visitation, indulged at Cambridge in a strong attack upon Evening Communions.—*Rock*, 1889, June 7th, p. 5.

(3) Approves Monastic Life.

(*a*) Gave sanction to four priests (Church of England) going into monastic life at Coveney.—*Rock*, 1889, July 26th, p. 14.

(4) Grants Dispensations.

(*a*) Granted a dispensation to the people of his diocese to eat meat during Lent.—*English Churchman*, 1892, p. 150.

(*b*) Granted dispensation from fasting during Lent to persons in St. Ives, Oldhurst, and Woodhurst, provided they recited one of the Penitential Psalms. —*Rock*, 1894, February 16th, p. 5.

RITUALISTIC APPOINTMENTS BY PAST AND PRESENT BISHOPS.

Date of Preferment.	Name.	Ritualistic Societies and Petitions.	Ritual.
	CANONS RESIDENTIARY.		
1873	E. C. Lowe	C.D.V.T.P.	*ep., inc., al.*
1892	Bishop Macrorie	C.	
	HON. CANONS.		
1868	A. R. Grant		*ep., inc., al.*
1872	J. W. Haddock	T.	
1878	J. W. Cockshott	C.	*ep., al.*
1878	J. H. Macaulay	D.V.T.P.	*ep.*
1881	A. R. Evans	V.T.P.	
1886	C. J. Betham	D.V.T.P.	*ep., al.*
1890	F. F. M. S. Thornton	C.T.	*ep., inc., c., al.*
1891	B. W. Randolph	C.	
1895	R. Tompson	C.D.V.T.P.	
1896	E. G Punchard	T.	*ep., inc., r., al.*
1896	F. E. Warren	C.P.N.D.V.P.	*ep., inc , r., al.*
1896	W. Cunningham	C.	*ep., inc , al.*
1898	F. H. Cox	T.	
1898	F. Watson	C.D.V.	*ep., inc.*
	EXAMINING CHAPLAINS.		
1886	V. H. Stanton	T.	
1888	H. P. Currie	C.C.	
1892	W. C. E. Newbolt	C.L.V.T.P.	
1896	W. H. Hutton	C.	

RITUALISTIC APPOINTMENTS—continued.

Date of Prefer- ment.	Name.	Ritualistic Societies and Petitions.	Ritual.
	CHAPLAINS.		
1887	G. R. Bullock-Webster	c.	
1886	A. R. Evans	v.t.p.	

BISHOP COMPTON'S APPOINTMENTS TO BENEFICES.

Living.	Incumbent.	Date of Appt.	Yearly Value. £	Popu- lation.	Ritualistic Societies and Petitions.	Ritual.
Biggleswade ...	W.P.Henderson	1890	230	4,943	c.c.p. ...	ep., mc., al.
Chesterton,St.Luke	A. J. Mickle- thwaite ...	1892	4	7,000	+.c.u.l. v.p.t.	ep., mc., r , al.
Downham	F.M.S.Thornton	1892	462	1,873	u.t. ...	ep., mc., r., al.
Fridaybridge ...	L. Clutterbuck	1888	200	616	c.u.l.n.v. t.p.	ep., mc , al.
Glemsford	H. Hall	1887	264	2,441	t.... ...	ep.
Harston	E. C. Baldwin .	1889	250	767	u.d.v.p. .	ep., mc., r., al.
Leverington ...	C. B. Drake ...	1896	300	574	v.t.	ep., mc., al.
Linton...	J. C. Longe ...	1887	180	1,753	... ...	ep.
Luton, St. Saviour	J. C. Trevelyan	1892	46	4,762	+.c.u. .	ep., mc., r., al.
Madingley	T. A. Lacey ...	1894	131	195	+.c.u.t.	ep., mc., r., al.
Pondsbridge ...	W.H. Hampton	1897	142	623	... ...	ep., mc., al.
Sudbury, St. Gregy.	B. S. Fryer ...	1893	318	3,646	. . ...	ep.
Swaffham Bulbeck	E. Singleton ...	1894	200	800	v.	
Teversham	J. R. L. Knipe .	1891	301	285	c.u. ...	ep., r., al.
Waterbeach... ...	J. Ross	1889	360	1,382	... ...	ep., mc., r., al.
Willingham ...	J. Watkins ...	1890	620	1,630	u.v.t.p .	ep., mc., al.
Cambridge,St.Giles	J. F. Buxton ...	1897	290	2,843	c.v.	ep., mc., v., al.
Total	... ...	£	4,298	36,133		

MASSES FOR THE DEAD.

The Bishop allows Requiem Masses for the dead, under the Guild of All Souls, to be publicly celebrated in the following Churches in his Diocese :—

St. Ethelbert's, Hessett. v., he.
St. John's, Little Ouse. v., he.
St. Luke's, Cambridge. v., s., he.
St. Mary's, Gamlingay. s., he.
St. Saviour's, Luton. v., s., me.
All Saints', Chellesworth. he.

All Saints', Lolworth. he.
All Saints', St. Ives', Hunts. he.
St. John's, Elmswell. he.
Holy Trinity, Ely. he.
St. Peter's, Prickwillow. he.

Bishop of Exeter, Dr. Bickersteth.

Salary, £4200 a year.

Consecrated 1885. Appointed by MR. GLADSTONE.

(1) Protects a Lawbreaker.

(*a*) In 1886 vetoed the prosecution of Mr. Tothill, notwithstanding his statement "to Mr. Tothill that they [the practices complained of] are in my judgment *contrary to the laws* and usages of the Church of England, and are therefore not only inexpedient but wrong."

(2) Invites Communicants to take part in lawlessness.

(*a*) Invited all communicants in Torquay to meet him in St. John's Church, Torquay, where coloured vestments are worn, and the vicar is a member of C. B. S. and E. C. U.—*English Churchman*, 1887, p. 688.

(3) Grants Dispensation.

(*a*) Dispensed certain "High Church" people in the three towns from fasting during Lent.—*English Churchman*, 1892, p. 235.

(4) Winks at Romanism and does nothing.

(*a*) In January, 1894, Captain Cobham called the Bishop's attention to the frequent erection of tabernacles for the reserved wafer in the Exeter Diocese, which his Lordship had power to stop; but no answer was vouchsafed. Twelve months later, the condition of the Diocese of Exeter became such that *The Record* said (June 21st), "It is notorious that Romanizing practices and distinctively Roman doctrines are observed and taught," and "conversions from within the most intimate clerical circles have taken place even from clerical families." But beyond verbal complaints, the Bishop has done nothing whatever.

RITUALISTIC APPOINTMENTS BY PAST AND PRESENT BISHOPS.

Date of Preferment.	Name.	Ritualistic Societies and Petitions.	Ritual.
	ARCHDEACON.		
1890	A. E. Seymour...	C.C.T.P.	*ep., al.*
	PREBENDARIES.		
1856	C. F. Smith ...	P.V.T.P.	*ep., al.*
1876	Earl of Devon...	...	*ep.*
1881	J. T. Pigot	V.T.P.	*ep.*
1885	E. N. Dumbleton	T.P.	
1885	F. C. Hingeston-Randolph	V.P.	*ep., al.*
1885	H. Tudor ...	D.T.P.	*ep.*
1889	R. J. Hayne ...	D. ...	*ep.*
1892	H. Bramley ...	D.P.	
1893	W. S. Boyle ...	...	*ep., al.*
1894	R. Martin ...	V.T.P.	*ep., me., al.*
	PRECENTOR.		
1889	B. M. Cowie	D.T.P.	*ep., al.*

RITUALISTIC APPOINTMENTS—continued

Date of Preferment.	Name.	Ritualistic Societies and Petitions.	Ritual.
	EXAMINING CHAPLAINS.		
1885	F. K. Aglionby...		ep., al.
1888	S. G. Ponsonby		ep., r., al.
	CHAPLAINS.		
1887	J. T. Pigot	V.T.P.	ep.
1888	R. J. Hayne	D. ...	ep.
1888	H. Bramley	D.P.	
1888	W. M. Birch	N.V.T.P. ...	ep.

BISHOP BICKERSTETH'S APPOINTMENTS TO BENEFICES.

Living.	Incumbent.	Date of Appt.	Yearly Value. £	Population.	Ritualistic Societies and Petitions.	Ritual.
Barnstaple, Hy. Ty.	E. C. Atherton	1893	122	2,761	c.v. ...	ep., mc., al.
Bridestowe	J. L. Francis .	1889	242	586	D.V.T.P.	
Farringdon	A. Gill	1889	321	130	... ...	ep., al.
Ilfracombe, Hy. Ty.	R. Martin ...	1887	258	5,295	V.T.P. ...	ep., mc., al.
Lynton...	W. E. Cox ...	1887	182	1,213	... .	ep., mc., al.
Sowton...	S. T. Serle ...	1889	182	410	v.	
Symbridge	J. F. L. Gueritz	1887	290	2,188	r.t. ...	ep., mc.
Yealmpton	G. G. Woodhouse	1888	197	932	... ...	ep.
Total	...		£1794	13,515		

MASSES FOR THE DEAD.

The Bishop allows Requiem Masses for the dead, under the Guild of All Souls, to be publicly celebrated in the following Churches in his Diocese :—

All Saints', Plymouth. v., s., HE.
St. James', Plymouth. v., s., HE.
St. Mary Steps, Exeter. v., s., HE.
St. Peter's, Plymouth. v., s., HE.

The Good Shepherd, Plymouth. v., s., HE.
St. Andrew's, Kenn. HE.
St. James', Avonwich. HE.
St. John's, Bovey Tracey. v., s., HE

Also a Requiem celebration for deceased members of E. C. U. at

St. James', Avonwich.
All Saints', Babbacombe.

All Saints', Torquay.
St. John's, Torquay.

Bishop of Gloucester, Dr. Ellicott.

Salary, £4300 a year and a Palace.

Consecrated 1863. Appointed by LORD PALMERSTON.

(1) Does nothing when appealed to.

(*a*) Notice of Ritualism at St. Simon's, Bristol. Communion administered with eight candles, incense, wafers, biretta, orange, crimson and gold cope during procession, chasuble afterwards, and notice given that the Holy Eucharist would be offeied up to commemorate the finding of the Holy Cross. Simply acknowledged; no action taken.—*English Churchman*, 1889, p. 561.

(2) Wears Popish Mitre.

(*a*) Used pastoral staff and mitre.—*Rock*, 1892, January 1st, p. 4; February 12th, p. 5.

(3) Reopens notorious Mass House.

(*a*) Consecrates St. Raphael's, Bristol. Pronounced Benediction holding pastoral staff.—*English Churchman*, 1893, p. 370.

(4) Hinders Protestantism.

(*a*) Prevented Rev. F. J. Horsefield from giving Protestant lecture at Fishponds, Bristol.—*Protestant Observer*, 1896, p. 3.

(5) Exercises his Veto to protect Lawbreakers.

(*a*) The Bishop exercised his Veto, wrongfully under the P. W. R. A. in order to protect the Rev. R. W. Randall from prosecution for Romish Ritual.

(*b*) He also exercised his Veto under the C. D. Act to protect the Rev. John Baghot de la Bere.

(6) Scandal lies at the door of the Bishop.

(*a*) At Lower Guiting, the church is in a "deplorable" condition. The vicarage has been turned into "the Monastery of St. Bernard." The clergy— the Rev. Dr. Green and Mr. Drake, better known as "Father" Green and Father Anselm, are Monks of the Order of St. Benedict, a Roman Catholic Order of which Mr. B. F. Carlyle is Prior; there is no congregation, and the churchwardens, after a long and bitter experience, during which they have not been able to get any help from the Bishop, are obliged to record in their last presentment that the fault of the present scandal is entirely the Bishop's (see *Cheltenham Free Press*, May 21st, 1898).

(7) The Bishop's Inconsistency.

This is the Bishop who complains that the Ritualists are "digging the grave of the Establishment"!

RITUALISTIC APPOINTMENTS BY PAST AND PRESENT BISHOPS.

Date of Preferment.	Name.	Ritualistic Societies and Petitions.	Ritual.

ARCHDEACON.

1882	H. R. Hayward	...	D.P. ...	ep., al.

HON. CANONS.

1878	T. G. Golightly	...	...	D.V.T.P.
1884	J. Mayne	...	...	D.P.
1893	T. Koblo	...	...	P.D.V.T.P.

CHAPLAIN.

1883	J. Mayne	...	...	D.P.

BISHOP ELLICOTT'S APPOINTMENTS TO BENEFICES.

Living.	Incumbent.	Date of Appt.	Yearly Value. £	Population.	Ritualistic Societies and Petitions.	Ritual.
Almondsbury	C. O. Miles	1888	286	2,000	c.u.v. ...	ep., mc., v. al.
Ashleworth	B. Edwards	1890	132	450	... ...	ep., mc.
Bedminster, St. Jn.	A. H. F. Burder	1888	250	15,000	v.v.t. ...	ep., mc., v. al.
Bishopworth, S. Pr.	W. Molesworth	1868	300	1,980	T.	
Bedminster, St. Fr.	W. H. Fisher	1886	190	5,500	... ...	ep.
Bishopston, St. My.	H. Ault	1886	210	500	c.	
Bishopston, St. Ml.	E. Evans	1888	300	6,000	... ...	ep., al.
Bream	E. F. Eales	1896	300	2,013	c.v.	ep., mc., al.
Bristol, St. Andrew, Montpelier	W. F. Steele	1881	244	6,500	... ...	ep., al.
Bristol, St. Barnab.	T. J. Weight	1890	294	6,344	... ...	ep.
Bristol, St. Mark, Lower Easton	T. H. Barnett	1873	267	8,000	... ...	ep.
Bussage	N. D. Macleod	1891	100	320	c.c. ...	ep., mc.v., al.,i.
Cam, Lower	A. F. S. Hill	1895	190	1,132	v. ...	ep., mc., v., al.
Charlton Kings, St. Mary	T. Hodson	1892	120	2,350	v.t. ...	ep., al.
Cheltenham, All St.	G. L. H. Gardner	1886	433	3,762	... ...	ep., v., al.
„ St. Stephen	E. L. Jennings	1890	330	1,385	... ...	ep.
Cirencester	H. R. Hayward	1881	211	7,500	d.p. ...	ep., al
Clearwell	C. F. Goddard	1895	278	1,000	... ...	ep., al.
Clifton, St. John	A. C. C. Anstey	1888	182	6,399	... ...	ep., al.
Coalpit Heath	F. W. Griffiths	1881	150	1,781	... ...	ep., al.
Coleford	A. W. Cornwall	1891	213	4,199	... ...	ep.
Deerhurst	D. G. Lysons	1893	280	712	v.t.	
Dursley	N. W. Gresley	1890	195	2,269	v.v.t. ...	ep., mc.
Edge	T. P. Little	1883	204	314	v.p.	
Gloucester, All St.	H. C. Foster	1884	310	5,859	... ...	ep., al.
Gloucester, S. Cath.	G. C. Keble	1890	332	3,186	... ...	ep.
Gloucester, St. Luke	H. Proctor	1895	250	6,000	... ...	ep., mc., al.
Gloucester, St. Paul	J. H. Owen	1894	140	3,302	t.p. ...	ep., mc., al.
Gloucester, St. Mark	S. E. Bartleet	1885	142	3,097	... ...	ep., mc., al.
Marston, South	A. Macdonald	1889	120	378	v. ...	ep.
Hinton, Little	R. E. Richards	1890	266	217	v.v. ...	ep.
Horfield	F. Bingham	1879	230	2,378	t.p. ...	ep., al.
Knowle, H. Nativity	G. Dunlop	1887	171	12,000	c.v.t. ...	ep., mc.v., al., i.
Newland	R. H. Evered	1895	270	616	v. ...	ep., mc., al.
Newnham-on-Severn	W. G. Baillie	1890	121	1,401	...	ep., mc.

APPOINTMENTS TO BENEFICES—continued.

Living.	Incumbent.	Date of Appt.	Yearly Value. £	Population.	Ritualistic Societies and Petitions.	Ritual.
Northleach	C. Hutchinson	1894	130	1,106	... ...	ep., c., al.
Oakridge	R. L. Simkin	1895	150	580	v. ...	ep., mc., al.
Oxenhall	J. H. Lorimer	1889	90	183	v.d.v.t.p.	
Pauntley	J. H. Lorimer	1889	66	180	v.d.v.t.p.	
Poulton	W. J. Mayne	1894	74	406	+ c.v.	ep., mc., r., al.
Sevenhampton	J. Storr	1890	134	399	... ...	ep., mc., al.
Standish	A. Nash	1889	284	489	... ...	ep., al.
Stroud, St.Law'nce	G. Fox	1891	237	4,875	T. ...	ep.
Stroud, H. Trinity	E. H. Hawkins	1879	394	4,031	v. ...	ep.
Swindon, St. Mark	M.J.G.Ponsonby	1879	283	16,000	c.v.t. ...	ep., al.
Swindon, St. Barnabas	P. Maddocks	1890	201	4,000	... ...	ep., al.
Swindon, St. Paul	D. P. Ware	1892	226	7,000	c.v. ...	ep., mc., r., al., i.
Whiteshill	J. F. Green	1883	120	1,691	d.t.p. ...	ep., mc., r., al.
Wroughton	J. R. Turner	1875	261	2,511	d.t.p. ...	
Total			£10661	169,325		

MASSES FOR THE DEAD.

The Bishop allows Requiem Masses for the dead, under the Guild of All Souls, to be publicly celebrated in the following Churches in his Diocese:—

St. Mary's, Prestbury. v.s., he.
St. Michael's, Bussage. v.s., he.
St. Michael's, Michaeldean. s., he.

St. Margaret's, Leigh Delamere. he.
St. Mary's, Kempley. he.
St. Michael's, Bishops Cleeve. he.

Also a Requiem celebration for deceased members of E. C. U. at St. Mary's, Prestbury.

Bishop of Hereford, Dr. Percival.

Salary, £4200 a year.

Consecrated 1895. Appointed by LORD ROSEBERY.

The Bishop has declared himself in favour of the proposed Romanist University for Ireland.

RITUALISTIC APPOINTMENTS BY PAST AND PRESENT BISHOPS.

Date of Preferment.	Name.	Ritualistic Societies and Petitions.	Ritual.
	CANONS RESIDENTIARY.		
1892	C. S. Palmer	P.D.T.P.	ep., mc., al.
1896	F. M. Williams	C.C.D.V.T.P. ...	ep., mc., v., al.
	PREBENDARIES.		
1880	E. F. Clayton	D.V.P.	
1881	C. Warner	P.D.V.T.P.	
1883	J. Burd	T.	
1886	M. H. Ricketts... ...	D.T P. ...	ep.
1886	T. A. Ayscough ...	U.	
1887	W. H. Lambert ...	U.L D.V.T.P. ...	ep., al.
1887	C. E. M. Green ..	... ...	ep., al.
1889	W. Elliot	U.D.V.T.P. ...	ep., al.
1890	C. S. Palmer	U.D.T.P. ...	ep., mc., al.
1892	W. Jellicorse	U.D.V.	
1892	A. L. Oldham... ...	V.T.	ep.
1892	F. M. Williams ...	C.U.D.V.T.P. ...	ep., mc., v., al.
1893	G. E. Ashley	U.D.V.P.	
1893	W. Rayson	U.D.V.T.P.	
1894	J. H. Brierley	D.P.	
1897	F. Burd...	T.P.	
	PRECENTOR.		
1889	J. Hampton ...		ep., mc., al.

BISHOP PERCIVAL'S APPOINTMENT TO A BENEFICE.

Living.	Incumbent.	Date of Appt.	Yearly Value. £	Population.	Ritualistic Societies and Petitions.	Ritual.
Bosbury	R. B. Bayly ...	1897	300	916	U.T.	ep.

MASSES FOR THE DEAD.

The Bishop allows Requiem Masses for the dead, under the Guild of All Souls, to be publicly celebrated in the following Churches in his Diocese :—

Holy Trinity, Minsterley. v., s., HE. | St. James the Great, Colwell. HE.
St. Luke's, Iron Bridge. HE.

Bishop of Lichfield, Dr. Legge.

Salary, £4200 a year.

Consecrated 1891.   Appointed by LORD SALISBURY.

(1) Grants Dispensation.
Offered to give dispensation from fasting to the visitors to St. Oswald's College, Ellesmere.—*Rock*, 1897, p. 695.

RITUALISTIC APPOINTMENTS BY PAST AND PRESENT BISHOPS.

Date of Preferment.	Name.	Ritualistic Societies and Petitions.	Ritual.
	CANON RESIDENTIARY.		
1888	C. Bodington	C.U.N D.V.P.	
	PREBENDARIES.		
1875	Bishop Sir L. Stamer	T	ep.
1880	W. Allen		ep., al.
1884	J. H. Lester		ep.
1885	W. Hutchinson	D.V.T.	ep., me.
1885	O. Dobree	C.D.V.	ep.
1888	G. W. Corbet	C.	
1890	H. Meynell	C.D.V.T.P.	
1894	R. Hodgson	D.V.T.P.	ep., me.
1895	H. Abud	C.	ep.
1895	C. N. Bolton		ep.
1896	A. Moncrief	C.U.L.T.P.	
1896	W. T. Burges	D.P.	
	EXAMINING CHAPLAIN.		
1891	H. L. Thompson	T.	
	CHAPLAINS.		
1891	M. M. Connor		ep.
1891	A. H. Talbot	C.P.T.	ep., me., r., al.

BISHOP LEGGE'S APPOINTMENTS TO BENEFICES.

Living.	Incumbent.	Date of Appt.	Yearly Value. £	Population.	Ritualistic Societies and Petitions.	Ritual.
Burton-on-Trent, St. Modwen	V. A. Boyle	1892	112	2,169		ep., al.
Criftins	W. R. Rugg	1894	110	800		ep.
Hanbury	E. C. Robinson	1893	173	1,122	r.	
Hamstead	J. H. Firminger	1895	150	1,100	r.	ep., me., a.l.
Hednesford	B. Holland	1894	357	10,293		ep., me., al.
Leek, St. Edward	T. H. B. Fearon	1896	320	6,108	V.T.P.	e.p
Longton, St. Jas.	R. H. Harris	1892	400	7,264		ep., me.
Longton, St. John	G. Oliver	1895	320	10,009	c.	ep., me., c., al.
Pelsall	W. Climpson	1894	270	3,800	C.P.T.	ep., me.
Ruyton-XI.-Towns	W. B Gowan	1892	235	1,113		ep., al.
Shrewsbury,S.Giles	F. Roberts	1894	170	750		ep., me.
Smethwick,H.Trin.	T. Ridsdel	1892	200	8,911	L.D.V.T.P.	ep.
Stafford, St. Chad	R. McCleverty	1893	220	500	c.v.	ep., al.

APPOINTMENTS TO BENEFICES—continued.

Living.	Incumbent.	Date of Appt.	Yearly Value. £	Population.	Ritualistic Societies. and Petitions.	Ritual.
Stafford, St. Mary	M. Scott	1894	182	1,149	... ...	ep., al.
Stone, St. Michael	A. E. B. Owen	1893	257	2,031	c. ...	ep., inc.
Tunstall, ChristCh.	H. R. Coldham	1895	255	10,000	... ...	ep.
West Bromwich, St. Peter	H. Jesson	1893	280	7,509	+.c.v.t.p.	ep., al.
Wolverhampton, St. Peter	A. Penny	1894	510	3,797	u.d.v.	ep., al.
Yoxall	A. A. Cory	1894	420	1,001	... ...	ep.
Pipe Ridware	E. Samson	1897	56	84	t.p.	
TOTAL			£ 4997	79,810		

MASSES FOR THE DEAD.

The Bishop allows Requiem Masses for the dead, under the Guild of All Souls, to be publicly celebrated in the following Churches in his Diocese:—

Sneyd Church, Burslem. v., s., ue. | St. Stephen's, Smethwick. v, s., ue.

Bishop of Lincoln, Dr. King.

Salary, £4500 a year.

Consecrated 1885. Appointed by Mr. GLADSTONE.

(1) **Takes part in rank Popery.**

(*a*) Preached 1888 at High Celebration at St. Agnes's, Kennington. Celebrant was robed in white chasuble, with deacon and sub-deacon in dalmatics and tunicles, and two acolytes in cassocks and albs. See also *Rock*, January 20th, 1888, p. 4. Made sign of cross before commencing sermon.—*English Churchman*, 1888, p. 40.

(*b*) Present at dedication of new church at Clumber by Bishop of Southwell, dressed in a cloth of gold cope. Took part in procession and recession. See p. 90.—*English Churchman*, 1889, p. 674.

(*c*) Reopened All Hallows, Clixby. Service "Low Mass." Celebrated, vested in cope and mitre. Roof of church adorned with monogram " M " with a crown. Lights and brass crucifix on retable. Procession headed by an acolyte carrying a large brass crucifix. Bishop in cope and mitre preceded by pastoral staff. See also *Protestant Observer*, 1889, p. 294.—*English Churchman*, 1889, p. 702.

(*d*) At dedication festival at St. Nicholas's, Searby, procession headed by cross, clergy in birettas, concluded by Bishop in cope and mitre. Prayers offered for the dead, and several hymns sung in honour of St. Nicholas.—*English Churchman*, 1889, p. 810.

(*e*) Preached at St. John the Divine's, Brixton. Five of the "six points" employed in the service. Made sign of the cross before the sermon.—*Rock*, 1890, January 17th, p. 5.

(*f*) Attended, January 19th, 1890, a dedication festival at St. Agnes's, Kennington. The service was a "Missa Cantata." Incense used. Banners, cross, and copes were used in the procession ; acolytes and thurifers attended upon the Bishop and clergy. See also *Rock*, 1890, January 24th, p. 5.—*English Churchman*, 1890, p. 42.

(*g*) Assisted at High Mass at St. Saviour's, Leeds. Crucifix, procession. Thurifer carrying the thurible. Incense-boat. Crucifer bearing aloft a large crucifix, two brazen images, one of Virgin Mary, the other of St. John, clergy in birettas, assisting priests in dalmatics, albs and stoles, celebrant in chasuble. Was escorted to the pulpit by a "Crucifer" (carrying a processional crucifix) and two boys in red cassocks and cottas. When censed he bowed at every swing of the thurible.—*English Churchman*, 1890, p. 677.

(*h*) The Bishop of Lincoln is a Vice-President of the Romanizing English Church Union.

RITUALISTIC APPOINTMENTS BY PAST AND PRESENT BISHOPS.

Date of Preferment.	Name.	Ritualistic Societies and Petitions.	Ritual.
	ARCHDEACON.		
1897	J. Bond...		*cp*.
	CANON RESIDENTIARY.		
1895	H. R. Bramley		U.N.V.P.

RITUALISTIC APPOINTMENTS—continued.

Date of Preferment.	Name.	Ritualistic Societies and Petitions.	Ritual.
	PREBENDARIES.		
1863	A. S. Wilde	...	ep.
1868	C. Nevile	T.P.	
1872	F. Hemmans	D.T.	ep.
1874	T. S. Nelson	...	ep.
1874	J. H. Crowfoot	T.	
1875	A. Wright	D.T.	
1875	R. Bullock	V.T.P.	ep., me., al.
1876	G. L. Hodgkinson	C.U.D.V.P. ...	ep., v., al.
1876	G. F. Deedes	D.T.P.	ep., me., al.
1877	C. E. Fisher	C.U.T.P.	ep., al.
1883	A. J. Ingram	... ...	ep., al.
1884	J. Bond	... ...	ep.
1884	F. B. Blenkin	... ...	ep.
1885	J. P. Young	U.D.V.P.	ep.
1885	J. G. Smyth	U.T.	ep., al.
1886	C. Wordsworth	D.V.T.	
1886	H. E. Tweed	V.T.	
1888	W. A. Brameld	C.U.T. ...	ep., v., al.
1888	S. W. Andrews	U.	ep., al.
1889	G. T. Harvey	U.V.T.P. ...	ep., me., v., al.
1890	W. Glaister	D.V.P. ...	ep., al.
1892	E. F. Quarrington	... ...	ep.
1895	R. E. Warner	C.U.L.D.V.T.P.	ep., me., v., al.
1896	H. Hutchinson	U.D.V.T. ...	ep., v.
1896	E. Wharton	C.V.T. ...	ep., v., al.
1897	G. W. Jendwine	D.V.T.	
1897	H. Footman	...	ep.
1897	J. Stephenson	...	ep.
1897	A. R. Maddison	U.V.P	
	EXAMINING CHAPLAINS.		
1885	H. K. Bramley	U.N.V.P.	
1890	B. W. Randolph ...	U.	

BISHOP KING'S APPOINTMENTS TO BENEFICES.

Living.	Incumbent.	Date of Appt.	Yearly Value. £	Population.	Ritualistic Societies and Petitions.	Ritual
Bardney	C. E. Laing ...	1896	200	1,393	C.U.T.	ep., me., v., al.
Barnethly-le-Wold	C. F. Brotherton	1892	321	852	v.	
Barton-on-Humber, St. Peter	H. G. C. North- Cox	1894	210	5,226	...	ep., me., al.
Bolingbroke, New.	H. S. Fawssett	1895	289	450	C.U.	ep., me., al.
Caistor, St. Paul ...	W. F. W. Westbrooke	1886	250	2,100	C.U.V. ...	ep., v., al., i.
Cleethorpes	H. Hutchinson	1895	137	20,000	U.D.V.T.	ep., v.
Clee, St. John ...	G. E. Mahon ...	1895	295	14,000	v.	ep., me., v., al.
Cockerington ...	G. Shaw	1887	105	216	...	ep., al.
Eastville	S. Hope	1890	280	1,197	v.	
Gainsborough, All Saints	C. Moor	1894	380	5,600	...	ep., me., v., al.

APPOINTMENTS TO BENEFICES—continued.

Living.	Incumbent.	Date of Appt.	Yearly Value. £	Population.	Ritualistic Societies and Petitions.	Ritual.
Gainsborough, Hy. Trinity	F. H. Dalby	1891	296	6,000	C.U.T....	ep., mc., v., al.
Gainsborough, St. John	F. C. Fisher	1896	126	4,500	C.U.T....	ep., mc., v., al.
Glamford Brigg	A. N. Claye	1893	187	3,100	U.	
Grimsby, St.Andw.	R. Meddings	1889	303	15,000	... ...	ep., al.
Huttoft	W. T. Jennings	1893	140	535	C.U. ...	ep., mc., v., al.
Lincoln, St. Andw.	J. E. Truman	1896	305	4,300	C.U. ...	ep., al.
Lincoln,St.Botolph	D. H. Ellis	1891	178	4,800	... ...	ep., v., al., i.
Lincoln, St. Martin	V. B. Lucas	1894	300	4,546	U. ...	ep., mc., al.
Lincoln, St.Swithin	W. Wanstall	1895	241	8,000	C.V.P....	ep., al.
Martin	J. H. Boldero	1895	183	777	... ...	ep., al.
Mumby, St. Peter	W. R. Stoyle	1895	210	374	... ...	ep., r., al.
Nettleham	B. W. Hancock	1890	250	918	C.C. ...	ep., v., al.
Rauceby	A. W. M. Drew	1888	186	658	... ...	ep.
Saxilby	E. A. Trasenster	1891	105	1,300	... ...	ep.
Stoke, North	R. E. Warner	1894	594	421	C.U.L.D. V.T.P.	
Hykeham	J. J. Baldwin	1897	193	499	C.U.	
TOTAL			£ 6264	106,762		

MASSES FOR THE DEAD.

The Bishop allows Requiem Masses for the dead, under the Guild of All Souls, to be publicly celebrated in the following Churches in his Diocese:—

St. Aidan's, Boston. s., HE.
Lenton Church, Grantham. v., s., HE.
St. Martin's, Welton, Louth. v., HE.

St. Peter and Paul, Caistor. v., s., HE.
All Saints', Nettleham. HE.

Also a Requiem celebration for deceased members of E. C. U. at
St. German's, Scothorne.

Bishop of Llandaff, Dr. Lewis.

Salary, £4200 a year.

Consecrated 1883. Appointed by MR. GLADSTONE.

(1) **Sanctions Mass Music for the Young.**
   (a) Opened a new clergy school at Aberdare. This college "insists on all its students learning sufficient of the theory and principles of music to enable them satisfactorily to celebrate High Mass" (*Musical Standard*, May 19th).— *English Churchman*, 1892, p. 223.

(2) **Supports the Romanizing E.C.U.**
   (a) Took the chair at an E.C.U. meeting at Cardiff. Lecturer, Rev. "Father" Puller, of Cowley.—*English Churchman*, 1896, p. 857.

RITUALISTIC APPOINTMENTS BY PAST AND PRESENT BISHOPS.

Date of Preferment.	Name.	Ritualistic Societies and Petitions.	Ritual.
	DEAN.		
1897	W. H. Davey		V.T.
	CANON RESIDENTIARY.		
1889	G. Roberts		V.V.
	HON. CANONS.		
1897	J. T. Harding	C.P.L.N.D.V.T.P. ...	ep., al.
1892	C. J. Thompson	T.	ep., mc.
	CHANCELLOR OF THE CATHEDRAL.		
1895	J. J. Lias	V.T.P.	
	EXAMINING CHAPLAINS.		
1887	J. J. Lias	V.T.P.	
1897	G. Roberts	V.V.	

BISHOP LEWIS'S APPOINTMENTS TO BENEFICES.

Living.	Incumbent.	Date of Appt.	Yearly Value. £	Population.	Ritualistic Societies and Petitions.	Ritual.
Abergavenny, Holy Trinity	J. R. Phillips ...	1893	290	3,500	... ...	ep., mc., al.
Bishopston	P. Potter ...	1891	230	628	D.V.N.P.	ep., mc.
Canton, St. John	A. Henderson	1894	370	38,000	... ...	ep., al.
Canton, St. Cathr.	J. Baker	1894	160	11,000	... ...	ep.
Canton, St. Paul	F. P. Hill ...	1894	60	17,000	... ...	ep.
Cardiff, All Saints	E. H. Hyslop	1890	220	6,000	... ...	ep.
Cymmerand ...	W. Thomas ...	1894	200	15,000	V.	
Cowbridge	D. Bowen ...	1886	246	768	...	ep.
Llanbrynmair ...	D. A. Jones ...	1894	239	1,530	V.	
Llanferris	O. B. Price ...	1897	231	560	T.	
Llanengan	H. G. Williams	1891	231	1,400	C.C.V.	
Llanfrechfa ...	R. W. B. Sanderson ...	1893	197	5,000	... ...	ep., al.

APPOINTMENTS TO BENEFICES—continued.

Living.	Incumbent.	Date of Appt.	Yearly Value. £	Population.	Ritualistic Societies and Petitions.		Ritual.
Mountain Ash ...	B. Lloyd ...	1884	300	13,449	...	...	ep., al.
Newcastle	D. Davies ...	1891	155	7,559	...	...	ep.
Pontypridd	J. P. Griffiths	1895	200	18,000	...	...	ep.
Pyle	T. M. Jones ...	1889	94	932	v.		
Roath, St. Saviour	J. E. Le Dawson	1893	78	12,000	c.v.	...	e.p., mc., v., al.
Llangwm	E. M. Prothero	1897	325	820	v.		
TOTAL			...£ 3826	153,146			

MASSES FOR THE DEAD.

The Bishop allows Requiem Masses for the dead, under the Guild of All Souls, to be publicly celebrated in the following Churches in his Diocese:—

St. Agnes', Roath. v., s., IIE.
St. German's, Roath. v., s., IIE.
St. John Baptist's, Newport, Mon. v., IIE.
St. Martin's, Roath. v., s., IIE.
St. Mary Virgin. Cardiff. v., s, IIE.

St. Mary's, Wenvoe. v., s., IIE.
St. Saviour's, Roath. v., s., IIE.
St. Canna's, Llangan, Bridgend. IIE.
St. Margaret's, Roath. IIE.

Also a Requiem celebration for deceased members of E.C.U. at
St. Mary's, Cardiff.

Bishop of Manchester, Dr. Moorhouse.

Salary, £4200 a year.

Consecrated 1876. Translated 1886 by LORD SALISBURY.

(1) The Bishop breaks his promise.

(*a*) On October 4th, 1894, promised at Blackburn that "he would at once cause any clergyman to obey the law as the Courts had declared it." On being furnished with formal evidence of such illegalities by parishioners of St. Alban's, Cheetwood, and St. Mark's, City Road, his Lordship made no reply, and did nothing.—*Church Intelligencer*, XII.

(*b*) On complaint being made of illegal practices at Stockport, he refers complainant to the Law Courts. On being asked if he would not veto proceedings under the P. W. R. Act, he vouchsafes no reply.

(*c*) The Bishop of Manchester has declared himself in favour of the proposed Romanist University for Ireland.

RITUALISTIC APPOINTMENTS BY PAST AND PRESENT BISHOPS.

Date of Preferment.	Name.	Ritualistic Societies and Petitions.	Ritual.
	ARCHDEACON.		
1895	A. F. Clarke	r. ...	*ep., al.*
	CANONS RESIDENTIARY.		
1884	J. D. Kelly	...	*ep., al.*
1892	E. L. Hicks	...	*ep., me.*
	HON. CANONS.		
1866	A. T. Parker	v p. ...	*ep., al.*
1878	J. Allen...	r.d.v.t.p.	
1890	J. H. Rawdon	... ...	*ep.*
1891	W. T. Jones	... ...	*ep., me., al.*
1892	J. Rogers	r.t.	
1893	J. J. Scott	...	*ep., me., al.*
1894	J. P. Rountree...	...	*ep., me.*
1894	St. V. Beechey, jun.	...	*ep.*
1895	J. G. Doman	t.	
1897	E. J. Russell	r.v.t.p. ...	*ep.*
	EXAMINING CHAPLAINS.		
1892	E. L. Hicks		*ep., me.*
1898	J. J. Scott		*ep., me., al.*

BISHOP MOORHOUSE'S APPOINTMENTS TO BENEFICES.

Living.	Incumbent.	Date of Appt.	Yearly Value. £	Population.	Ritualistic Societies, and Petitions.	Ritual.
Bamford	F. C. Dearden .	1892	206	1,898	...	*ep.*
Bolton-le-Moors, St. Peter	E. Hoskyns ...	1895	670	7,899		*ep.*
Bolton-le-Moors, Holy Trinity ...	T. T. Evans ...	1890	350	9,267	t.	*ep., me.*

APPOINTMENTS TO BENEFICES —continued.

Living.	Incumbent.	Date of Appt.	Yearly Value. £	Population.	Ritualistic Societies and Petitions.	Ritual.
Bolton-le-Sands, Holy Trinity ...	S. V. Beechey	1890	166	1,365	... ...	ep.
Burnley, St. Andw.	C. Jones... ...	1894	252	15,125	... ...	ep.
Castleton, AllSaints	R. Hartley ...	1896	200	3,000	c.	
Hatcliffe	J. Pickop ...	1888	200	165	t. ...	ep., mc., al.
Heaton Norris, Christ Church .	G. C. Little ...	1892	292	9,348	... ...	ep., mc.
Heaton Norris, All Saints ...	R. Masheder ...	1891	270	7,020	... ...	ep., mc.
Hindsford	C. Bromley ...	1892	150	3,000	t.	
Manchester, St. Anne	D. Dorrity ...	1895	250	435	... ...	ep.
Manchester, St. Simon	W. Burns ...	1895	250	2,391	... ...	ep., al.
Norwell	W. Russell ...	1895	161	532	c.	
Dearnley, S. Andw.	G. R. Oakley...	1895	240	2,100	... ...	ep., mc.
Rochdale, St. Luke	A. D. Davies...	1895	300	5,000	... ...	ep.
Total			£ 3957	68,545		

MASSES FOR THE DEAD.

The Bishop allows Requiem Masses for the dead, under the Guild of All Souls, to be publicly celebrated in the following Churches in his Diocese :—

St. Gabriel's, Hulme. HE. | St. Matthew's, Burnley. HE.

Also a Requiem celebration for deceased members of E.C.U. at

St. Benedict's, Ardwick. | St. Mark's, City Road.
St. Gabriel's, Hulme. |

Bishop of Newcastle, Dr. Jacob.

Salary, £3400 a year and a Palace.

Consecrated 1896. Appointed by LORD SALISBURY.

RITUALISTIC APPOINTMENTS BY PAST AND PRESENT BISHOPS.

Date of Preferment.	Name.	Ritualistic Societies and Petitions.	Ritual.
	HON. CANONS.		
1882	T. Brutton	V.T.	ep., r., al.
1887	H. S. Hicks	...	ep.
1889	J. H. Usher	T.	
1890	H. F. Long	U.V.T.	ep., me., al.
1890	J. Henderson	...	ep., al.
1891	O. Churchyard	+.C.U.	ep., me., r., al.
1892	G. Robinson	+.C.U.D.V.P.	ep., me., r., al.
1894	E. J. Gough	C.U.T.	ep.
1894	S. R. Coxe	U.D.T.	
1896	J. M. Lister	C.U.D.T.P.	ep., me., al.
1897	J. Walker	U.V.P.	
1897	S. Jeffrey	T.	
1897	E. M. Young	...	ep.
	EXAMINING CHAPLAINS.		
1892	J. Henderson		ep., al.
1896	E. M. Young		ep.
	CHAPLAIN.		
1896	E. J. Gough	C.U.T.	ep.

BISHOP JACOB'S APPOINTMENT TO A BENEFICE.

Living.	Incumbent.	Date of Appt.	Yearly Value. £	Population.	Ritualistic Societies and Petitions.	Ritual.
Benwell, St. James	H. Bott	1896	200	16,000		r.

MASSES FOR THE DEAD.

The Bishop allows Requiem Masses for the dead, under the Guild of All Souls, to be publicly celebrated in the following Churches in his Diocese :—

Cramlington Church. s., ne.
St.John Evangelist's,Greenside,Ryton-on-Tyne. v., ne.
St.Luke's,Newcastle-on-Tyne. v.,s.,ne.
St. Philip's, Newcastle - on - Tyne. v., s., ne.

Seghill Church. v., s.
St. Wilfrid's, Newcastle - on - Tyne. v., s., ne.
St. John Baptist's, Ulgham. ne.
St. Stephen's, Seaton Delaval. ne.

Also a Requiem celebration for deceased members of E.C.U. at
St. John Baptist's, Ulgham.

Bishop of Norwich, Dr. Sheepshanks.

Salary, £4500 a year and a Palace.

Consecrated 1893. Appointed by MR. GLADSTONE.

(1) His antecdents.

(*a*) The Bishop is an ex-Member of the Romanizing E. C. U.

RITUALISTIC APPOINTMENTS BY PAST AND PRESENT BISHOPS.

Date of Prefer- ment.	Name.	Ritualistic Societies and Petitions.	Ritual.
	ARCHDEACON.		
1894	Bishop A. J. Lloyd	D.V.T.P.	
	HON. CANONS.		
1856	H. Howell	T.P.	
1881	J. M. Du Port	V.D.V.T.P.	ep., me., al.
1892	F. B. De Chair	T.	
1897	E. G. A. Winter	T. ...	ep.
	EXAMINING CHAPLAIN.		
1893	H. F. Chenevix-Trench	C.V.V.	ep., me., al.

BISHOP SHEEPSHANKS' APPOINTMENTS TO BENEFICES.

Living.	Incumbent.	Date of Appt.	Yearly Value. £	Popu- lation.	Ritualistic Societies and Petitions.	Ritual.
Belton	W. Leeper	1895	290	752	V.T.	ep., me., al.
Heigham, St. Bart.	D.W. Mountfield	1895	212	11,000	...	ep., me.
Kessingland	F. W. R. Mason	1894	311	1,454	T.	ep., me.
King's Lynn, All St.	A. H. Hayes	1895	246	5,088	V.	ep., al.
Norwich, St. Geo., Tomblands	W. F. Crewe	1895	70	780	C.V.T. ...	ep., me., al.
Thetford, St. Cuth.	E. H. Love	1894	12	1,628	...	ep., v. al.
Coston	F. E. New	1897	96	242	V.	
TOTAL			£1237	20,944		

MASSES FOR THE DEAD.

The Bishop allows Requiem Masses for the dead, under the Guild of All Souls, to be publicly celebrated in the following Churches in his Diocese :—

All Saints', Ellough. v., ne.
St. Andrew's, Earl's Framlingham. v., s., ne.
St. Bartholomew's, Ipswich. v., s., ne.
St Bartholomew's, Shipmeadow. v., ne.
St. Michael-at-Plea, Norwich. v., s., ne.
Kirkley Church, Lowestoft. ne.
St. Mary Virgin, Pulham, St. Mary. ne.
St. Mary's, Ufford, Woodbridge. v., s., ne.
St. Mary's, West Tofts. v., ne.

Also a Requiem celebration for deceased members of E. C. U. at St. John, Maddermarket.

Bishop of Oxford, Dr. Stubbs.

Salary, £5000 a year.

Consecrated 1884. Translated 1888 by LORD SALISBURY.

(1) Does nothing when appealed to.

(a) CHIPPING-NORTON.—Colonel Dawkins complained of elevation of alms by vicar. The Bishop did nothing.—October 22nd, 1893.

(b) Holy Trinity, Reading. Memorial of Parishioners complained that Choral Communion was announced in *The Parish Magazine* to be celebrated "not for receiving the Sacrament." Bishop Stubbs merely scolded the Memorialists.—*English Churchman*, June 25th, 1896.

(2) His antecedents.

(a) The Bishop is an ex-Member of the Romanizing E. C. U.

RITUALISTIC APPOINTMENTS BY PAST AND PRESENT BISHOPS

Date of Preferment.	Name.	Ritualistic Societies and Petitions.	Ritual.
	ARCHDEACONS.		
1880	Bishop Randall	V.P.	
1869	A. Pott	D.P.	*ep.*
1895	C. F. J. Bourke	C.D.V.T.P.	
	HON. CANONS.		
1867	A. Pott	D.P.	*ep.*
1870	T. T. Carter	+.C.U.N.V.P.	
1874	A. P. Purey-Cust	T. ...	*ep.*
1876	J. Slatter	...	*ep.*
1880	T. Evetts	U.V.	*ep., al.*
1880	F. Menzies	T.	
1881	E. Savory	...	*ep., al.*
1884	N. T. Garry	D.V.T P.	*ep., me.*
1890	W. F. Norris	D.T.P.	*ep., me., e., al.*
1892	W. Wood	D.T.P.	
1892	H. Blagden	V.P.	
1892	J. Wood	L.D.V.T.P.	
1895	W. M. G. Ducat	T. ...	*ep., me., al.*
1895	J. H. Thompson	C.D.V.T.P.	*ep., al.*
1895	E. E. Holmes	C.U.	
1896	E. Sturges	D.V.T.P.	*ep., me., al.*
	EXAMINING CHAPLAINS.		
1889	J. O. Johnston	...	*ep., me., al.*
1893	R. C. Moberley	C.D.V.T.P.	
	CHAPLAINS.		
1888	Chancellor Espin	...	*ep., me., al.*
1888	Dean Gregory	D.T.P.	*ep., al.*
1889	Dean Paget	T. ...	*ep., al.*
1889	Archdeacon Barber	C.U.V.T.P.	*ep., me., e., al*
1895	R. L. Ottley	C.U.	
1884	E. E. Holmes	C.U.	

BISHOP STUBBS'S APPOINTMENTS TO BENEFICES.

Living.	Incumbent.	Date of Appt.	Yearly Value. £	Population.	Ritualistic Societies and Petitions.	Ritual.
Abingdon, St. Helen	W. Watson	1896	161	6,501	C.U.S.V.	ep., mc., r., al.
Ascot-under-Wychwood	C. Walford	1893	200	421	... ...	ep., al.
Aston Rowant	F. M. Sparks	1893	115	601	... ...	ep., al.
Aylesbury	C. O Phipps	1895	365	6,642	U. ...	ep., mc., al.
Baldon Toot	A. E. Caldecott	1894	236	270	U. ...	ep., mc., al.
Blewbury	E. I. Gillam	1895	227	620	... ...	ep.
Cranborne, St. Pet.	R. A. Hamilton	1891	209	1,142	...	ep., mc., al
Crowthorne	G. F. Coleridge	1894	173	2,000	U. ...	ep., mc., al.
Cuddesdon	J. O. Johnston	1894	201	450	... ...	ep., mc., al.
Filkins	G. V. Proctor	1893	175	470	V.T. ...	ep., mc., al.
Fonthill Bishop's	W. M. Bone	1892	145	164	U.V.T. ...	ep., mc., al.
Greenham	H. H. Skrine	1890	88	660	T.	ep., mc., al.
Hailey	H. Wilson	1893	245	818	...	ep., mc., al.
Headington Quarry	C.F.H. Johnston	1891	131	1,307	U.V.	ep., mc.
Hendred, East	H. Lewis	1890	380	815	...	ep., v., al.
Hook Norton	A. W. Russell	1894	200	1,263	...	ep., al.
Kidmore End	J. E. Smith-Masters	1889	218	735	C.U.	ep., mc., r., al.
Lambourn	R. Bagnall	1895	125	1,600	U. ...	ep., al.
Langford	C.G. Wodehouse	1893	213	424	U.N.D.V.T.P	
Launton	W. M. Miller	1895	520	619	V.T. ...	ep., mc., al.
Linslade	C. E Dandrige	1892	160	1,982	... ...	ep., v., al.
Liscard	J.H D.Cochrane	1886	400	6,000	...	ep.
Maidenhead, S. Lk.	H. G. J. Meara	1890	376	5,465	V.D.P.	ep., mc.
Malford Christian	J. Mayne	1890	600	570	D.P.	
Marlow, Gt., H.Ty.	H. O. F. Whittingstall	1890	197	5,000	...	ep., al.
Marsh Gibbon	E. R. Massey	1893	386	695		ep., mc., r.
Milton - under - Wychwood	D.H.W.Horlock	1895	260	1,128	U.	ep., mc., al.
Mixbury	R. R. Kirby	1891	210	240	U.D.T.P.	ep., al.
Patney	P. H. Jackson	1890	129	106	V.T. ...	ep., al.
Hawrridge	W. S. Norris	1897	150	214	U.	
Pusey	F. D. DeFreville	1889	151	117	...	ep., al.
Reading, St. Giles	W. M. G. Ducat	1894	130	16,000	T.	ep., mc., al.
Shippon	H.W. McCreery	1889	96	173	T.	ep., r., al.
Littlewick	T. H. Wrenford	1894	300	450	T.	ep., mc., al.
Earley, St. Barth.	S. J. Norris	1890	234	6,000	...	ep., mc., r., al.
Stewkley	R. B. Dickson	1890	252	1,328	T.P.	ep.
Stony Stratford, St. Giles	J. H. Light	1895	280	2,019	...	ep., mc., al.
Streatley	J. R. Izat	1892	245	607	P.T. ...	ep., mc., al.
Taplow	W. G. Sawyer	1890	450	961	U.D.V.T.P.	ep., mc., al.
Tew, Little	J. B. Jerwood	1895	123	250	... ...	ep., al.
Slough, St. Mary	P. H Eliot	1893	336	7,500	... ...	ep., al.
Wallingford, St. Leonard	E. B. Mackay	1892	180	1,228	C.U.	ep., mc., r., al.
Watlington	S. C. Saunders	1895	240	1,673	... ...	ep., r., al.
Reading, St. Mary	W. Neville	1897	440	14,000	C U.	ep., mc.
Taplow	N. T. Garry	1897	450	961	D.V.T.P.	ep., mc., al.

TOTAL ... ... £ 11102 102,189

MASSES FOR THE DEAD.

The Bishop allows Requiem Masses for the dead, under the Guild of All Souls, to be publicly celebrated in the following Churches in his Diocese:—

St. Agnes', Spital. v., s., he.
St. Mary and John, Oxford. v., he.
St. Mary's, Addington, Bucks. v., s., he.
St. Mary's, Freeland. v., he.
St. Olave's, Fritwell. v., he.

St. Peter and Paul, Dorchester, Oxon. v., s., he.
St. Stephen's College Oratory, Clewer. v., s., he.
St. Nicholas', Hedsor. he.

Also a Requiem celebration for deceased members of E. C. U. at
St. Mary's, Souldern.

Bishop of Peterborough, Dr. Carr Glyn.

Salary, £4500 a year.

Consecrated 1897. Appointed by LORD SALISBURY.

RITUALISTIC APPOINTMENTS BY PAST AND PRESENT BISHOPS.

Date of Preferment.	Name.	Ritualistic Societies and Petitions.	Ritual.
	ARCHDEACONS.		
1880	R. P. Lightfoot		ep., al.
1886	Bishop Mitchinson		ep., mc.
	CANONS RESIDENTIARY.		
1880	R. P. Lightfoot		ep., al.
1890	F. C. Alderson	V.T.P.	ep.
	HON. CANONS.		
1885	H. S. Syers	D.P.	
1889	W. B. Beaumont		ep., al.
1890	S. J. W. Sanders		ep., mc.
1890	J. Denton		ep.
1891	C. R. Ball	V.T.P.	
1893	J. E. Stocks	V.D.V.T.P....	ep.

MASSES FOR THE DEAD.

The Bishop allows Requiem Masses for the dead, under the Guild of All Souls, to be publicly celebrated in the following Churches in his Diocese :—

St. Barnabas', Wellingborough. V., HE.
St. Laurence's, Northampton. V., S., HE.
St. Luke's, Wellingborough. V., HE.
St. Paul's, Leicester. V., HE.

Thornton Church, Leicester. V., S.
All Saints', Wellingborough. HE.
St. James', Thurning, Oundle. HE.
Bagworth Church, Leicester. HE.

Also a Requiem celebration for deceased members of the E. C. U. at

Holy Cross, Bagworth. | St. Peter's, Thornton.

Bishop of Ripon, Dr. Boyd Carpenter.

Salary, £4200 a year.

Consecrated 1884. Appointed by MR. GLADSTONE.

RITUALISTIC APPOINTMENTS BY PAST AND PRESENT BISHOPS.

Date of Preferment.	Name.	Ritualistic Societies and Petitions.	Ritual.
	CANON RESIDENTIARY.		
1884	M. MacColl	U.D.V.T.P.	
	HON. CANONS.		
1889	F. J. Wood	U.D.V.P. ...	ep., me., al.
1893	F. G. H. Smith ...	U.D.V.P. ...	ep., me., al.
1895	J. Eddowes	U.D.V.T P.	ep., al.

BISHOP BOYD CARPENTER'S APPOINTMENTS TO BENEFICES.

Living.	Incumbent.	Date of Appt.	Yearly Value. £	Population.	Ritualistic Societies and Petitions.	Ritual.
Bleasby	H. L. Williams	1881	300	296	T.	
Bradford, St. Thos.	C. Briggs ...	1890	232	5,608	U.	
Bradford, St. Bart., Bowling	T. Kruckenberg	1888	200	4,827	U.	ep.
Brigsley	A. H. Askey ...	1893	39	140	U.	
Caunton	J. Tinkler ...	1891	193	395	U.L.V.D.P.	ep., me., r., al.
Eastgate	J. G. B. Knight	1894	390	329	T.	ep., al.
Kippax	E. B. Smith ...	1896	266	3,727	U.	ep., me., al.
Middleham ...	W. Kerr-Smith	1894	292	732	...	ep., al.
Riddlesden ...	H. A. Claxton	1895	159	758	...	ep.
	TOTAL	...	£2071	16,812		

Bishop of Rochester, Dr. Talbot.

Salary. £4100 a year.

Consecrated 1895. Appointed by LORD SALISBURY.

(1) Takes part in Romish Practices.

(*a*) Held a confirmation at St. George's, Sydenham. Procession in church headed by processional crucifix, followed by acolytes, clergy and banner of the "Patronal Saint."—*Protestant Observer*, 1896, p. 52.

(*b*) Took part in service at St. Agnes', Kennington, bowed repeatedly to the Lord's Table and to an incense bearer, who censed Bishop, clergy and two side altars. Wore a large gold cross, walked in procession, with large cross on a pole seven or eight feet high borne in front.—*Rock*, 1896, p. 164.

(*c*) Held an ordination at St. Mark's, Kennington, *an Evangelical Church*, on Sunday, September 20th. Wore a mitre, cope, jewelled cross, &c. Pronounced the Benediction holding his pastoral staff.—*English Churchman*, 1896, p. 660.

(*d*) Took part in service at which a cross was carried in procession at St. Paul's, Deptford.—*Protestant Observer*, 1897, p. 45.

(*e*) Consecrated St. Alphege, Southwark, attired in a white cope, and wore his mitre. Celebrated communion. Sacring bell rung at consecration prayer. —*English Churchman*, 1897, p. 326.

The Bishop of Rochester has declared himself in favour of the proposed Romanist University for Ireland.

(2) Gives no Redress to Protestant Complaints.

(*a*) Complaint of Ritualism, hymns to Virgin, vestments, &c., at St. Ann's, South Lambeth Road. Bishop replied upholding the vicar.—*Protestant Observer*, 1896, p. 156.

(3) Encourages a Romanizer.

(*a*) Appointed Canon Bristow, c.u.s., as Missioner for the Diocese.—*Protestant Observer*, 1897, p. 31.

RITUALISTIC APPOINTMENTS BY PAST AND PRESENT BISHOPS.

Date of Preferment.	Name.	Ritualistic Societies and Petitions.	Ritual.
	ARCHDEACON.		
1879	C. Burney		*cp.*
	HON. CANONS.		
1877	F. W. Murray	U.V.T P.	*cp., al.*
1878	J. Scarth	T P.	*cp., al.*
1878	H. F. Phillips	V.T.P.	
1880	E. Daniel		*cp.*
1881	C. T. Procter	V.T.P.	*cp., al.*
1890	G. T. Palmer		*cp.*
1890	C. F. Grant	V.T.	*cp., al.*
1892	R. R. Bristow	C.V.L.V.P.	*cp., r., al.*
1893	J. R. Nicholl	P D.V.T P.	*cp., mc.*
1894	E. J Beck	D.V.T.P.	*cp., al.*

RITUALISTIC APPOINTMENTS—continued.

Date of Preferment.	Name.	Ritualistic Societies and Petitions.	Ritual.
	EXAMINING CHAPLAIN.		
1895	W. H Frere ...	c.	
	CHAPLAIN.		
1895	R. S. Hunt	C.D.V.T.P ...	ep., al.

MASSES FOR THE DEAD.

The Bishop allows Requiem Masses for the dead, under the Guild of All Souls. to be publicly celebrated in the following Churches in his Diocese :—

All Hallows, Southwark. v.
St. Alphege's, Southwark. v., s.
St. Anselm's, Streatham. v., s.
The Ascension, Lavender Hill. v., l.
St. John Evangelist, East Dulwich. v., s.
St. Katherine's, Rotherhithe. v., s.
St Peter's, Streatham. v., s.

St. Michael's, Wandsworth Com. he.
St. Michael and All Angels, Woolwich. he., l.
St. Paul's Mission, Streatham. he.
The Transfiguration, Lewisham. he.
St. Stephen's, Lewisham. v.
All Saints', Walworth. he.

Also a Requiem celebration for deceased members of E. C. U. at Christ Church, Clapham.

Bishop of Salisbury, Dr. John Wordsworth.

Salary, £5000 a year.

Consecrated 1885. Appointed by LORD SALISBURY.

(1) Makes overtures to the enemy.

(*a*) In 1894 published a Latin letter to the Jansenist Bishop of Utrecht, claiming that English presbyters are sacrificing priests, and that Article XXXI. does not condemn the Roman Mass.—*Church Intelligencer*, XII.-5.

(*b*) In 1895 he wrote a preface to the book written by two members of the C. B. S. and S. S. C., and published at the expense of the E. C. U., for presentation to the Pope, making the same claim and a like profession of identity in doctrine with Rome as to the Mass. As to "Transubstantiation," it said, the Church of England "vocabulum quidem rejicit; nec tamen doctrinam."— *Church Intelligencer*, XII.-122.

RITUALISTIC APPOINTMENTS BY PAST AND PRESENT BISHOPS.

Date of Preferment.	Name.	Ritualistic Societies and Petitions.	Ritual.
	ARCHDEACONS.		
1874	T. B. Buchanan	T.P.	
1875	F. Lear	D.T.P.	
	CANONS RESIDENTIARY.		
1862	F. Lear	D.T.P.	
1895	T. B. Buchanan	T.P.	
	PREBENDARIES.		
1861	E. P. Eddrup	D.V.T.P.	*ep., al.*
1870	Sir J. E. Phillipps	C.D.T.P.	
1872	H. T. Glyn	V.P.	
1874	R. Lowndes	...	*ep.*
1874	D. Olivier	C.P.T.	*ep.*
1874	F. Warre	...	*ep., al.*
1875	T. L. Kingsbury	T.P.	
1876	R. S. Hutchings	...	*ep.*
1876	J Duncan	V.P.	*ep., al.*
1881	J. J. Jacob	V.T.P.	
1889	E. Inman	D.V.T.P.	
1890	E. E. Dugmore	C.C.L.V.T.P.	*ep., mc.. r ,al., i.*
1892	Hon. S. Meade	C.P.T.	
1893	W. Gilden	...	*ep.*
1894	Hon. B. P. Bouverie	...	*ep.*
1895	C. H. Mayo	C.V.T.P.	
1896	S. E. Davies	C.V.T.	*ep., mc.*
1896	H. C. Powell	T.P.	*ep., mc., al.*
	SUB-DEAN.		
1887	G. H. Bourne	T.P.	
	EXAMINING CHAPLAINS.		
1885	F Lear	D.T.P.	
1896	H. J. C. Knight	...	*ep., mc.*
	CHAPLAINS.		
1886	C. Myers	V. ...	*ep., mc., r., al.*

BISHOP WORDSWORTH'S APPOINTMENTS TO BENEFICES.

Living.	Incumbent.	Date of Appt.	Yearly Value. £	Population.	Ritualistic Societies and Petitions.	Ritual.
Beaminster	A. A. Leonard..	1890	235	1,915	... ...	ep.
Boscombe,St.And.	H. W. Barclay..	1891	178	112	c.t.	
Bridport	H. R. W. Farrer	1895	256	3,768	... ...	ep., mc., al.
Broadwindsor	G. C. Hutchings	1895	121	1,105	v. ...	ep., mc.
Burbage	W. A. Heygate.	1890	73	1,060	... ...	ep., mc., al.
Charminster	C. L. Dundas...	1895	257	1,779	v.t.p. ...	ep., mc., al.
Chideock	E. H. Greenhow	1895	125	633	v.	ep., mc.
Durnford	L. Selby	1897	270	419	v.	
Easterton	G. A. King	1895	220	582	v.	ep., mc.
Fordington,St.Geo.	S. Boulter	1888	237	2,850	c.v.t.	ep.
Gillingham	S. E. Davies	1891	206	3,909	v.v.t.	ep., mc.
Lavington	R. W. Allsopp..	1892	243	1,086	v.l.t.p.	ep., mc., al.
West Lulworth	W. P. Schuster	1887	111	415	v.t.	
Lyme Regis	C R. H. Hill...	1891	215	2,365	... ...	ep., al.
Marlborough, St. Peter	C. Wordsworth.	1897	207	1,300	d.v.t.	ep., mc., al.
Marlborough, St. Mary	Bishop Mylne...	1897	169	1,845	v.v.s.	ep., mc., al.
Mere	J. A. Lloyd	1890	209	2,279	v.t.	ep., mc., al.
Motcombe	S. Dugdale	1892	236	1,309	... ...	ep.
Netheravon	A. D. Clutsom .	1895	174	374	c.	ep., mc.
Osmington	E. J. Bodington	1894	147	295	... ...	ep., mc.
Potterne	E. Inman	1891	217	1,154	d.v.t.p.	ep.
Poulshot	T. B. Buchanan	1891	286	316	t.p.	ep., mc.
Preshute	W. G. Hubbard	1886	117	800	c.v.	ep., mc., al.
Preston	E. J L. B. Henslowe	1891	208	678	... ...	ep.
Salisbury,St.Edm.	J. D. Morrice..	1890	309	3,649	v.t. ...	ep.
„ St.Martin	C. Myers	1894	218	6,410	v.	ep., mc., r., al.
Shrewton	C. V. Goddard..	1895	153	548	... ...	ep., mc.
Upwey	F. B. Howell...	1889	331	730	c.v.v.t.	ep.
Verwood	C. Brown	1887	133	1,190	+.c.r.	ep., mc., r., al.
Westbury,All Snts.	P. M. Smythe...	1890	349	3,500	v. ...	ep., mc., r., al.
Weymouth,H.Trin.	L. B. Weldon...	1894	77	5,000	v. ...	ep., mc., al.
Whitechurch Canonicorum	C. Druitt	1891	326	1,235	c v.v.t.	ep.,mc.. v., al.
Wool	A. C. B. Dobie.	1896	122	509	t.	ep.
Warminster	H.R.Whytehead	1897	415	3,770	v.t.	ep., mc., al.
Total			£ 7150	58,889		

MASSES FOR THE DEAD.

The Bishop allows Requiem Masses for the dead, under the Guild of All Souls, to be publicly celebrated in the following Churches in his Diocese :—

The Ascension, Woodlands.   v., s., he. | St. James's, Cherhill, Calne.   s., he.
St. James and Clement, Alderholt. | All Saints', Chardstock.   he.
s., he.

Also a Requiem celebration for deceased members of E. C. U. at St. James's, Holt.

Bishop of Southwell, Dr. Ridding.

Salary, £3500 a year.

Consecrated 1884. Appointed by MR. GLADSTONE.

(1) Dedicates Popery.

(*a*) Dedicated new church at Clumber. Over rood screen a gigantic crucifix is erected ; on either side images of Virgin Mary and St. John. Very large crucifix over " High Altar." Tabernacle for the reserved sacrament. Procession headed by crucifer bearing large crucifix, a thurifer bearing a censer, two acolytes bearing candles. Two banners, one of " Blessed Sacrament," *i.e.*, wafer, other of Virgin Mary. On this latter one were the words " S. Maria Mater Dei." Pastoral staff of Southwell; he himself wearing a gorgeous cope of many colours. On the back was a picture in brilliant colours of the Madonna and Child—a crown on her head, but none on that of her Divine Son. Many illegal ceremonies, &c., &c. See also *Rock*, January 31st, 1890, p. 5, and *Protestant Observer*, 1889, p. 284.—*English Churchman*, 1889, p. 674.

(*b*) In 1895 took part in the dedication services at St. Agatha's, Landport, including a Lady altar surrounded by "various scenes from the life of our Lady, and the high altar decorated with a picture of a priest saying Mass for the dead while angels bear the soul aloft." His Lordship bent in acknowledgment of the waft of incense.—*Church Times*, November 1st, 1895.

The omission of the Confession, Absolution, Prayer of Humble Access, and one or two parts of the prescribed Office was another feature in this lawless function.

(2) Defends Popery.

(*a*) In 1890 defended the rector of Killamarsh for elevating the Host, using incense, kneeling before the elements immediately after the consecration of each ; and misrepresented the facts pertinent to the complaint of the parishioners, whom he scolded for complaining.—*Church Intelligencer*, VII., 51-2.

(*b*) In 1897, when complaint was made by the Chairman of the Council of the C. A. as to the celebration of High Mass at Sneinton before the Church Congress with vestments, lights, elevation, incense, sacring, and the rest of the Roman ritual, the Bishop defended the practices on the ground that ritual " in itself " means nothing.

(3) No redress for complainants.

(*a*) Notice of introduction of Ritualism, vestments, wafers, elevation, &c., in Killamarsh Church, Chesterfield. No alteration made.—*English Churchman*, 1890, p. 69.

(*b*) ILKESTONE.—Messrs. Whitehead and Scott complained that vicar would not present for confirmation without confession. Bishop did not reply. April, 1897.

Mr. Scott complained, November, 1897, of High Mass and Eucharist for departed. No answer.

(*c*) Hon. Col. Coke complained of Ritualistic practices in Longford Church, but got no help from Bishop

(d) Notice of Holy Eucharist celebrated on All Souls' Day for all the departed souls at Holy Trinity, Ilkeston. Complaint ignored.--*English Churchman*, 1897, p. 789.

(4) His inconsistency.

(a) He told the Canterbury Convocation that " he believed that the objectionable practices of the extreme Ritualists were really directed by Secret Societies."
—*Guardian*, 1898, p. 768.

A reference to the Bishop's appointments (see below) will show how he has selected members of these Secret Societies for promotion.

RITUALISTIC APPOINTMENTS BY PAST AND PRESENT BISHOPS.

Date of Preferment.	Name.	Ritualistic Societies and Petitions.	Ritual.
	ARCHDEACON.		
1894	J. G. Richardson ...		ep., al.
	HON. CANONS.		
1885	J. J. Trebeck	V.P	ep., al.
1885	Bishop Were . .	...	ep.
1885	J. J. Singleton	r....	ep., al
1885	J. C. Massey ...	U.D.V.T.P.	
1885	A. F. Ebsworth	C.U.V.P. ...	ep., mc., r., al.
1886	C. Gray... ...	C.U.D.V.T.P.	ep., mc., r., al.
1888	N. Keymer . .	C.U.N.D.V.P.	ep., mc., r., al.
1888	G. E. Mason .	T.	ep., mc., v., al.
1891	J. M. Dolphin . .	U.V.T.P. ...	ep., mc., al.
1893	G. H. Sing . .	T. ...	ep.
1894	N. Madan ...	V.P.	
1894	W. D. B. Cator .	U.D.T.	
1894	Hon. C. J. Littleton . .	U....	ep., r., al.
1897	T. B. Ferris	...	ep.
1897	J. H. Godber	D.V.P.	
	EXAMINING CHAPLAINS.		
1884	Bishop Were	...	ep.
1884	G. H. Sing	T. . .	ep.
1894	Archdeacon J. G. Richardson	...	ep., al.

BISHOP RIDDING'S APPOINTMENTS TO BENEFICES.

Living.	Incumbent.	Date of Appt.	Yearly Value. £	Population.	Ritualistic Societies and Petitions.	Ritual.
Bampton, St.Thos.	H. E. Ferry ...	1896	236	8,130	C.U.T.	ep., mc., al.
Chesterfield, St. Mary	C. J. Littleton	1893	274	11,000	U.	ep., al., r.
Derby, St. Werburgh	Bishop of Derby	1889	450	4,800	... ...	ep.
Derby,St.Barnabas	F. P. Evans ...	1895	260	5,000	. . . .	ep., mc.
Derby, St. James..	W. H. M. Hills	1894	225	10,000	... ...	ep.
Derby, St. Luke...	R. H. S. Currey	1895	240	9,632	+. C.U.	ep., mc., r., al.
Derby, St. Michael	H. R. Rolfe ...	1885	174	781	C.V.T. ...	ep., r., al.
Derby, St. Thomas	F. J. Adams ..	1890	190	7,000	... ...	ep.
Donisthorpe ...	E. B. Lavies ...	1885	200	3,000	C.T.	
Eaton, Long ...	J. M. Dolphin	1890	270	9,636	U.V.T.P.	ep., mc., al.
Harby	A. Fraser ...	1885	174	320	T.	
Ilkeston,HolyTrin.	J. E. H. Binney	1892	160	5,000	C.U. ...	ep., r., al.

APPOINTMENTS TO BENEFICES—continued.

Living.	Incumbent.	Date of Appt.	Yearly Value. £	Population.	Ritualistic Societies and Petitions.	Ritual.
Mansfield, St. Mark	A. G. Henley	1893	150	3,820	v. ...	ep., mc., r., al.
Melbourne	J. J. Singleton	1888	395	3,369	v. ...	ep., al.
Newark,St.Leonard	H. B. McM. Holden ...	1890	122	2,740	v.t.	em., mc., r., al.
Nottingham. St. Mary	J. G. Richardson	1886	1,100	3,705		ep., al.
Nottingham, St. Catharine ...	C. E. Lewis ...	1894	230	3,780	v. ...	ep., mc., al.
Risley	J. C. Massey ...	1891	330	248	v.d.v.t.p.	
Sneinton,St.Maths.	W. H. C. Malton	1892	200	7,356	+. v....	ep., mc., r., al.
Stanley	H. L. Day ...	1896	140	1,001	v.	
Thorpe - by - Ashbourne	T. W. Windley	1888	105	190	...	ep., mc., al.
Whittington - with-Sheepbridge ...	J. Tomlinson ...	1892	325	6,388	t.	ep., mc., al.
Total ...			£5950	106,896		

MASSES FOR THE DEAD.

The Bishop allows Requiem Masses for the dead, under the Guild of All Souls, to be publicly celebrated in the following Churches in his Diocese :—

St. Anne's, Ambergate, Derby. s., he.
St. Anne's, Buxton. v., he.
St. Anne's, Derby. v., s., he.
St. Chad's, Stuffynwood. v., s., he.
St. John Baptist's, East Markham. v., s., he.
St. Katharine's, Teversal. v., he.
St. Matthias's, Nottingham. v., s., he.

St. Alban's, Nottingham. he.
St. Martin's, Bole. he.
St. Mary Virgin, Egmanton. he.
St. Michael's, Derby. he.
St. Michael's, Hoveringham. he.
St. Peter's, Bothamsall. he.
St. Peter's, Thurgarton. he.
St. Mary Virgin, Cumber Park. he.

Bishop of St. Albans, Dr. Festing.

Salary, £3200 a year.

Consecrated 1890. Appointed by LORD SALISBURY.

(1) Offers Prayers for the Dead.
(a) Present at a service held in St. John's, Red Lion Square, when Prayers for the Dead were publicly offered.—*English Churchman*, 1893, p. 26.
(a) Took part in service (Mass?) for repose of soul of late F. J. Ponsonby. *English Churchman*, 1894, p. 167.

(2) Complainants get no redress.
(a) Complaint of Romish teaching and hiding ten commandments at Dunmow. No action taken.—*Rock*, 1894, August 31st, p. 5.

(3) Uses unauthorized services.
(a) Used at ordination service at St. Michael's, Bishop Stortford, a service with altered rubrics, ordering elements to be " presented " and calling the Lord's table an " altar."—*English Churchman*, 1894, p. 878.
(b) At the Parish Church hid the Manual Acts, mixed water with the wine during service at Holy Table : both illegal acts.—May 18th, 1897.

(4) Approves Cowley Fathers.
(a) " Visitor " of Redcliffe House of Training for Women Missionaries. The warden is a Cowley Father, " S. S. J. E." (See p. 114.)—*English Churchman*, 1897, p. 793.

(5) A sample of what the Bishop sanctions in his Diocese.
(a) At St. Stephen's, Upton Park, Mass vestments are used, and there is an altar, altar lights, the seven lamps, an altar cross, a processional cross, red, white and green silk embroidered chasubles, red silk chalice-veil and burse, three pairs of altar vases.
(b) At St. Andrew's, Plaistow, " Vespers of the blessed Sacrament " are said, confessions are heard, the Sarum Ritual is used, altar lights are used, Romish vestments worn, the mixed chalice, sign of the cross, wafer bread, elevation of the elements, incense.
(c) At St. Mary's, Ilford, the Rev. A. Ingleby boasted that he had holy Mass, incense, holy water stoups, that he belonged to the C. B. S. and the Holy Rosary Society, that he has lights, crucifix, images, lamps, lady altar, processions, copes, stations of the cross. He is successor to Rev. A. S. Barnes, the author of *Ceremonial of the Altar*, a guide to low Mass, in which directions are given to pray for the Pope as *our* Pope in the Canon of the Mass.
(d) Consecrated St. Margaret's, Leytonstone. Vestments worn day after. Cross and " Mass Lights."—*English Churchman*, 1893, p. 83.

(6) How Romanism is supported by the Bishop.
(a) Out of 627 Benefices in the Diocese, 211 have Romish practices, and forty-four of these are in the gift of the Bishop,
(b) Out of £7317 raised by the Bishop of St. Albans Fund in one year, the

Bishop sanctioned £5013 being given in support of lawless clergy. A further sum of £4939 was devoted to the building of churches in which Romish practices were in use.

RITUALISTIC APPOINTMENTS BY PAST AND PRESENT BISHOPS.

Date of Prefer- ment.	Name.	Ritualistic Societies and Petitions.	Ritual.
	ARCHDEACONS.		
1884	W. J. Laurance	V.T.P.	ep.
1894	T. Stevens	...	ep., mc., al.
1894	Bishop H. F. Johnson	U.D.T.	
	HON. CANONS.		
1872	E. Hill	U.P.	
1877	O. W. Davys	V.T.P.	ep.
1877	P. G. Medd	D.V.P.	
1881	L. Hensley	...	ep.
1886	R. T. Whittington	D.V.T.P.	
1886	W. Wigram	U.T.	
1890	C. F. Norman	U.V.	ep., al.
1890	J. W. Irvine	T.	ep., mc.
1893	D. Ingles	U.T P.	ep., mc.
1894	J. C. Buckley	...	ep.
1897	W. Quennell	...	ep.
1897	J. D. Nairne	V.T.	ep., al.
1897	J. R. Corbett	U.V.T.P.	ep., al.
	EXAMINING CHAPLAINS.		
1890	J. H. Maude	U.	
1890	F. Watson	U.D.V.	ep., mc.
	CHAPLAINS.		
1891	H. T. Lane	V	ep., mc., r., al.
1897	H. H. Henson	...	ep., mc., al.

BISHOP FESTING'S APPOINTMENTS TO BENEFICES.

Living.	Incumbent.	Date of Appt.	Yearly Value. £	Popu- lation.	Ritualistic Societies and Petitions.	Ritual.
Asheldham	J. Cornah	1893	237	170	...	ep , mc., al.
Ashwell	S. W. P. Webb	1892	345	1,568	...	ep.
Baldock	J. D. Nairne	1893	210	2,000	V.T.	ep., mc., al.
Great Bentley	F. P. H. Powell	1894	291	1,003	V.	ep., r.
Little Burstead	A.W.Antenbring	1894	275	352	...	ep., mc., al.
Chelmsford, St. Mary	H. A. Lake	1895	65	4,837	C.U.T.	ep., mc., al.
Colchester, St. Jas.	C. C. Naters	1895	185	1,852	U.	ep., mc.
Forest Gate, All Saints	T.F.F.Williams	1895	390	7,000	...	ep., al.
Ham, St. Stephen, Upton Park	E. N. Powell	1891	200	23,000	U.	ep., mc., r., al.
Ham, St. Thomas	J. W. Eisdell	1893	200	6,000	...	ep., mc., al.
Kelvedon,St. Mary	E. F. Hay	1891	285	1,565	...	ep.
Leigh	R. S. King	1892	382	1,761	U.	ep., al.

APPOINTMENTS TO BENEFICES—continued.

Living.	Incumbent.	Date of App'.	Yearly Value. £	Population.	Ritualistic Societies and Petitions.	Ritual.
Leytonstone, St. Margaret	E. Sant	1893	150	6,000	v.	ep., mc., v., al.
Leytonstone, St. Columba	P. Barnes	1895	235	15,000	...	ep., mc., al.
Harrow Green, H. Trinity...	C. H. Rogers	1893	300	14,619	U.T.	
Tiptree Heath	F. H. Buckham	1896	293	880	+.c.U.T.	ep., mc., v., al.
Upton Cross, St. Peter	A. Durrant	1894	150	8,045	... ...	ep.
Colchester, St. Mary	G. T. Hales	1897	210	2,830	v. ...	ep., mc.
Laindon	H. Carpenter	1897	500	415	U.T.	ep., mc., al.
Halstead, H. Trin.	J. B. Oldroyd	1897	250	2,869	U.T.	ep., mc.
TOTAL			£5,063	101,766		

MASSES FOR THE DEAD.

The Bishop allows Requiem Masses for the dead, under the Guild of All Souls, to be publicly celebrated in the following Churches in his Diocese:—

St. Philip's, Plaistow. v., s., HE.
St. Thomas Martyr, Brentwood. v., HE.
All Saints, Southend-on-Sea. v., s., HE.
St. James's, Littleheath. v., HE.
St. Mary's, Little Braxted. v., HE.
St. Michael and All Angels', Walthamstow. HE.
St. Stephen's, Upton Park. HE.
St. John Baptist's, Harlow. HE.
St. Mary's, Panfield. HE.
St. Paul's, Colchester. HE.

Also a Requiem celebration for deceased members of the E. C. U. at St. Saviour's, Hitchin.

Bishop of St. Asaph, Dr. Edwards.

Salary, £4200 a year.

Consecrated 1889. Appointed by LORD SALISBURY.

RITUALISTIC APPOINTMENTS OF THE PAST AND PRESENT BISHOPS.

Date of Preferment.	Name.	Ritualistic Societies and Petitions.	Ritual.
	HON. CANONS.		
1892	H. Roberts...	...	*ep.*
1897	B. O. Jones	T.	
	CHAPLAIN.		
1889	G. W. Gent	r.	

BISHOP EDWARDS'S APPOINTMENTS TO BENEFICES.

Living.	Incumbent.	Date of Appt.	Yearly Value. £	Population.	Ritualistic Societies and Petitions.	Ritual.
Berriew	W. L. Martin...	1894	233	1,747	D.V.T.	
Hope	T. E. Jones ...	1891	359	2,612	V.T. ...	*ep.*
Colwyn Bay	H. Roberts ...	1893	120	4,000	... ...	*ep.*
Llanfyllin	T. Jones ...	1891	386	1,774	... ...	*ep.*
Llangernyw	D. Jones ...	1891	263	450	... ...	*ep.*
Llangollen	B. Jones ...	1895	210	5,643	... ...	*ep., al.*
Murchwiel	E. R. James ...	1895	423	648	V.T.P. ...	*ep.*
Rhyl	D. Edwards ...	1892	275	6,794	... ...	*ep.*
Gresford ...	E. A. Fishbourne	1897	593	1,814	V.T. ...	*ep., mc.*
TOTAL			£2,862	25,482		

Bishop of Truro, Dr. Gott.

Salary, £3000 a year.

Consecrated 1891. Appointed by LORD SALISBURY.

He speaks of "Altars" in the Church of England!!
(a) Asked clergy "how many servers they have at their altar?"—*English Churchman*, 1894, p. 639. (See also p. 103.)

RITUALISTIC APPOINTMENTS BY PAST AND PRESENT BISHOPS.

Date of Preferment.	Name.	Ritualistic Societies and Petitions.	Ritual.
	ARCHDEACONS.		
1888	J. R. Cornish ...	... ...	ep.
1892	H. H. Du Boulay	C.D.T.P. ...	ep., al.
	CANONS RESIDENTIARY.		
1885	A. B. Donaldson	C.D.V.T.P.	
1887	A. J. Worlledge	D.T.	
	HON. CANONS.		
1878	A. C. Thynne ...	C.U.T. ...	ep., r., al.
1878	J. R. Cornish ...	...	ep.
1878	C. F. Harvey ...	C.U.T. ...	ep., mc., r., al.
1881	W. P. Chappell	V.T.P. ...	ep.
1882	P. Bush ...	U.D.T.P. ...	ep., al
1882	H. H. Du Boulay	U.D.T.P. ...	ep., al.
1883	F. Hockin	U.T.P.	
1885	J. H. Moore ...	D.V.P.	
1885	J. S. Tyacke ...	... ...	ep.
1888	T. Hullah	... ...	ep., mc., al.
1889	V. H. Aldham ...	V.T. ...	ep., al.
1890	W. F. Everest ...	C.L.D.V.P.	
1892	J. Hammond ...	P.T.	ep., mc.
1892	G. H. Whitaker	T.	
1892	C. E. Hammond	C.U.N.D.V.P.	ep., mc., al.
1893	J. B. Jones	C.U.L.P. ...	ep., al.
1895	F. J. Bone	... ...	ep.
1895	E. Townend	U.	
1896	S. R. Flint	U.V.	ep.
	EXAMINING CHAPLAINS.		
1891	Canon Scott Holland ...	U.	
1891	J. R. Cornish ...	...	ep.
1891	Canon Worlledge	D.T.	
1894	G. H. Whitaker	T.	
	CHAPLAINS.		
1895	J. H. Moore ...	D.V.T.	
1891	A. C. Thynne ...	C.U.T.	ep., r., al.

BISHOP GOTT'S APPOINTMENTS TO BENEFICES.

Living.	Incumbent	Date of Appt.	Yearly Value. £	Population.	Ritualistic Societies and Petitions.	Ritual
Lawhitton	H. H. Du Boulay	1892	321	361	v.d.t.p.	ep., al.
Lezant	E. Townend	1896	101	680	v.	ep. me., v., al.
Looe	A. L. Browne	1896	160	2,401	v.	ep., al.
Newlyn, East	F. J. Bone	1892	315	120	...	ep., me.
Penzance, St. John	T. F. Maddrell	1896	318	4,576	c.v.	ep. me., v., al.
St. Colan	C.J.L.Lavanchy	1892	102	222	...	ep.
St. Enoder	W. Horsburgh	1892	227	1,120	c v l.n.v.p.	ep., me., al.
Saltash	A. Preedy	1895	305	2,745	c.v.	ep., me., v., al.
Truro	F. E. Gardiner	1897	90	2,500	t.	ep., me., al.
Total			£ 2239	14,725		

MASSES FOR THE DEAD.

The Bishop allows Requiem Masses for the dead, under the Guild of All Souls, to be publicly celebrated in the following Churches in his Diocese :—

St.Bartholomew's,Porthleven. v., s., he.
St. Clederus', St. Clether, Launceston.
   v., he.
St. Peter's, Newlyn. v., he.

Holy Trinity, Penponds, Camborne.
   v., s., he.
St. Dominic's, Cornwall. he.
St. Paul's, Truro. he.

The Bishop of Wakefield, Dr. Eden.

Salary, £3000 a year and a Palace.

Consecrated 1890. Translated 1897 by LORD SALISBURY.

The Bishop of Wakefield has declared himself in favour of the proposed Romanist University for Ireland.

RITUALISTIC APPOINTMENTS BY PAST AND PRESENT BISHOPS.

Date of Preferment.	Name.	Ritualistic Societies and Petitions.	Ritual.
	ARCHDEACONS.		
1888	J. I. Brooke	V.T.P.	ep., mc., al.
1892	W. Donne	T.	ep.
	HON. CANONS.		
1888	J. I. Brooke	V.T.P.	ep., mc., al.
1888	J. Sharp	C.P.D.V.T.P.	ep., mc., r., al.
1888	G. Sowden	P.D.V.T.P....	ep., al.
1888	W. W. Kirby	... ...	ep., al.
1891	W. S. Turnbull	P.D.V.T.P.	ep.
1892	W. Donne	T. ...	ep.
1893	H. L. Clarke	... ...	ep.
1895	F. R. Grenside	C.P.V.T.P....	ep., mc., al.
	EXAMINING CHAPLAINS.		
1888	Archdeacon Brooke	V.T.P.	ep., mc., al.
1888	W. F. Norris, Jun.	...	ep., mc., al.
1890	A. W. Robinson	...	ep., mc., al.

MASSES FOR THE DEAD.

The Bishop allows Requiem Masses for the dead, under the Guild of All Souls, to be publicly celebrated in the following Churches in his Diocese:—

All Saints', South Kirby. v., ne.
St. Andrew's, Netherton. v., s., ne.
House of Mercy, Horbury, v., ne.
St. Michael's, Halifax. v., s., ne.
St. Michael's, Wakefield. v., s., ne.

St. Peter's, Barnsley. v., s., ne.
St. Peter's, Horbury. v., s., ne.
St. Luke's, Middlestown. ne.
St. Paul's, East Thorpe, Mirfield. ne.

Nature and Objects of the Societies* and Petitions marked in the Lists.

(1) **THE SOCIETY OF THE HOLY CROSS.**—The members of this Society have the symbol + attached to their names. The names have been taken from the official and secretly printed Rolls of Brethren for 1897. This Society is composed of clergymen only, or *bonâ fide* candidates for Holy Orders. It is, in the strictest sense of the word, a *secret* Society. At the request of this Society a book was printed, and afterwards circulated by it, entitled *The Priest in Absolution*, of which the late Archbishop of Canterbury (Tait) said, in the House of Lords, on June 14th, 1877, that, "No modest person could read the book without regret, and that it is a *disgrace to the community* that such a work should be circulated under the authority of clergymen of the Established Church." On July 6th, in the same year, his Grace, in a speech delivered in the Upper House of Convocation, declared of the Society of the Holy Cross itself that it is,—"A conspiracy in our body against the doctrine, the discipline, and the practice of our Reformed Church." †

Episcopally-appointed Incumbents who are, or have been, members of this Society, are receiving £1401 every year to instruct 38,930 souls.

(2) **CONFRATERNITY OF THE BLESSED SACRAMENT.**—Members of this Society are marked C. in the lists. The names of the members are taken from the official *Roll of Priests-Associate for* 1896, which is the latest known to have fallen into Protestant hands. If any of those clergymen mentioned as members have withdrawn since 1896, they must blame the C. B. S. itself for the facts not being known to the compiler. If there is one thing more than another which the Society dreads, it is that Protestant Churchmen shall know the names of its Priests-Associate. In fact, some of those priests are so afraid of the light, that they will not allow their names to be printed at all, even in the privately issued Roll, in which it is stated : "There are in addition certain Priests-Associate who do not wish their names to appear in print." A secret "Intercession Paper" is circulated among the members every month, and no one is admitted to its Annual Meeting in London, unless he first of all produces his medal of membership. The chief objects of the Confraternity of the Blessed Sacrament are the propagation of belief in the Mass, and the "Real" Presence, together with Fasting Communion, Prayers for the Dead, the Reserved Sacrament, and the reunion of the Church of England with the Church of Rome. Writing to the "Superior General" of the Confraternity as to its work, the late High Church Bishop Wilberforce said : "It is quite sure to stir up a vast amount of prejudice from *its singularly un-English and Popish tone* . . . and as Bishop I exhort you to use no attempts to spread this Confraternity among

---

* For further information concerning these and other Ritualistic Societies, see Walsh's *Secret History of the Oxford Movement*. Price, post free, 11s.

† For a list of members of this Society, see *Church Association Tract, No. 244.* Price 1d.

the clergy and religious people of my diocese" (*Life of Bishop Wilberforce*, Vol. III., p. 71).*

Episcopally-appointed Incumbents who are members of this Society, are receiving £15,672 from their livings, and 261,393 souls are placed under their care.

(3) **ENGLISH CHURCH UNION.**—Members of this Society have the letter U. attached to their names. The names of members have been taken from the official *English Church Union Directory* for 1898. The Union has officially approved of the restoration of the Eastward Position, Popish Vestments, Lights in the daytime, and the Mixed Chalice and Unleavened Bread in the Protestant Church of England (*Church Union Gazette*, Vol. VI., p. 202). Moreover it has *officially* advocated, by the speeches of its President and in its Annual Report for 1878, the "restoration of *visible* communion" between the Church of England and the Church of Rome. Its deadly hostility to every existing authority in the Church, and support of law-breakers, is well known to almost everybody. Writing to the Rev. J. Bond, under date, December 22nd, 1870, the then Bishop of Bath and Wells thus referred to the E. C. U.: "My principal hope is in the good sense of clergy and laity discountenancing the proceedings of the English Church Union, *which will destroy the English Church* if they are encouraged in their present course." †

Episcopally-appointed Incumbents who are members of this Society, are receiving £47,001 per annum from their livings, and the very large number of 760,033 souls are placed under their care.

(4) **PETITION FOR LICENSED CONFESSORS.**—Those who signed this Petition have the letter L. attached to their names. The names are taken from a list printed at the time the Petition was presented. The petitioners not only asked "for the education, selection, and licensing of duly qualified Confessors" in the Church of England, but also for the Restoration of the "Reserved Sacrament," and Extreme Unction; and "the use of Processional Crosses and Banners, Credence Tables, Chalice Veils, Coloured Altar Cloths, and the like," together with other Popish rites.

(5) **CONFRATERNITY OF THE BLESSED SACRAMENT DECLARATION, IN FAVOUR OF NON-COMMUNICANT ATTENDANCE AT HOLY COMMUNION.**—Those who signed this Declaration have the letter N. following their names. It is stated in a "Note" to the *official* list of those who signed (London Hayes, 1872), that—"The Declaration has only been *privately circulated* amongst members of the C. B. S. and their friends and not advertised in the public prints." None but those in full sympathy with Sacerdotalism could sign such a very Popish Declaration The reasons why the Ritualists advocate Non-Communicant Attendance are very clearly explained in

---

* For a list of the members (about 1700) of this Confraternity, see Walsh's *Secret Work of the Ritualists*, published by the Church Association. Post free, 2½d.

† This Union claimed in 1897 to have 4279 clerical members, of whom 32 are Bishops. The names of the members are not published, but only printed for secret circulation.

the following quotation from one of their most popular manuals of devotion:—
" *Q.* If we are not going to communicate, ought we to go out of the Church before the Communion? *A.* No, we should stay to worship our Lord, even if we are not about to receive His Body and Blood, and should never leave at any rate until after the Consecration, *because the Sacrifice is not offered at all until then*" (*The Altar Manual,* 35th Thousand, 1877, p. 161). We thus learn the real object of Non-Communicant Attendance, namely, that those who remain may assist at, and receive the alleged benefits of, the Mass, or Sacrifice then supposed to be offered.

(6) **DECLARATION OF THE THREE DEANS.**—Those Clergymen who signed this Declaration are marked D. Their names are taken from the original List of Signatures. The Declaration is in favour of the Eastward Position and Vestments.

(7) **PETITION TO CONVOCATION.**—The letter V. is attached to the names of those who signed this Petition to the Convocation of Canterbury. It was presented in the year 1875. The names are taken from the list published by the English Church Union. The petitioners begged for the "retention" of the Sacrificial Vestments.

(8) **PETITION FOR TOLERATION OF EXTREME RITUAL.**—Those who signed this Petition are marked T. The names are taken from Bosworth's *Clergy Directory for* 1882. The Petition was presented in 1881. Those who signed it, state that, in their opinion, "The recognised toleration of *even wide* diversities of Ceremonial is alone consistent with the interests of true religion." Well might the ultra Romanizing *Church Review* remark of one who signed the Memorial, that it alone proved that, "he does not despise Ritual, *and he evidently loves the brethren*"* (February 8th, 1884, p. 61).

(9) **REMONSTRANCE AGAINST THE PURCHAS JUDGMENT.**—The letter P. is attached to the names of those who signed this Remonstrance. The names are taken from the official list published by Parker, London. Those who signed this document alone, and are not members of Ritualistic Societies, are not named in the lists. The object of the Remonstrance was to protest against the Purchas Judgment, because it condemned the Eastward Position.

SUMMARY OF STATISTICS.—461 Incumbents have (in one or the other of the ways indicated in these lists) publicly supported the Ritualistic movement, receiving through their livings, the sum of £118,356 per annum, and have 1,879,787 souls handed over to their care!

*The population of the parishes, and the annual income of the livings are quoted, with a few exceptions, from the "*CLERGY LIST*" for 1898. The compiler has taken the greatest care to be accurate, but should any inaccuracy be detected he begs to be corrected.*

* Nevertheless it is readily admitted that many of the signatories may not have appreciated the full scope and tendency of the Petition to which they were appending their names.

Extracts from Books Publicly Recommended by the Bishops to Candidates for Holy Orders.

THE PARISH PRIEST OF THE TOWN. By the Right Rev. JOHN GOTT, D.D., Bishop of Truro. First Edition.

[Recommended by the Bishops of Bath and Wells, Chester, Manchester, Southwell, St. Albans, Truro, and Wakefield.]

THE BIBLE SOCIETY.—" Don't join Dissenters on religious platforms; . . . it is wrong in principle, e.g., you will soon be asked to attend a meeting of the Bible Society. . . . The Church is the Bible Society. . . . Therefore I cannot go to a Bible Society, which annuls its own teaching, discredits its true witness, and does not know its own keeper" (pp. 153, 154).

ABSOLUTION.—" In the Absolution speak as one who bears the priceless Atonement from the God of penitents to the souls He has trusted to your care " (p. 180).

" EXCEPTIONALLY VALUABLE " BOOKS FOR THE CLERGY.—Bishop Gott gives in this *Parish Priest of the Town*, a list of books for a "Town Curate's Book-Shelf." He writes: "A fairly complete list would be cumbersome, and I only write down those that *I have found exceptionally valuable to myself*" (p. 211). Amongst the books thus highly commended—and the recommendation is now, alas! endorsed by *seven* Bishops—are *The Priest's Prayer Book* (p. 216); and Dr. Pusey's *Manual for Confessors* (p. 229). The former of these has forms of prayer for driving the devil out of salt and water, and a host of other superstitions, together with the most advanced Popery to be found within the Church of England. The latter work, for Father Confessors is outrageously Popish, being, in fact, translated, with adaptations. from a genuine Popish book by the Abbé Gaume.

THE TRUTH AND OFFICE OF THE ENGLISH CHURCH. By E. B. PUSEY, D.D. Fourth Thousand.

[Recommended by the Bishop of Lincoln.]

REUNION WITH ROME.—" I have never expected to see that external unity of intercommunion restored in my own day; but I have felt it to be an end to be wished for, and prayed for. I doubt not that the Roman Church and ourselves are kept apart much more by that vast practical system which lies beyond the Council of Trent, things which are taught with a quasi-authority in the Roman Church.

than by what is actually defined . . . explanations which, so long as they remain individual, must be unauthoritative, might be formally made by the Church of Rome to the Church of England, as the basis of Reunion " (pp. 98, 99).

INTERCESSION OF SAINTS.—" The mere 'ora pro nobis,' so explained, could not have led any to stop short in the Saints, nor have called forth any protest, out of zeal for God's honour " (p. 101).

PURGATORY.—" There is no ground for thinking that, in rejecting the popular 'Romish doctrine of Purgatory,' the Church of England meant to reject all suffering after this life."

ANOINTING OF THE SICK.—" Nor do I know of any ground, except the custom of the Church, why it should not be used in England " (p. 222).

TRANSUBSTANTIATION.—" My own conviction is, that our Articles deny Transubstantiation in one sense, and that the Roman Church, according to the explanation of the Catechism of the Council of Trent, affirms it in another " (p. 229).

STUDIES IN THE HISTORY OF THE BOOK OF COMMON PRAYER. By H. M. LUCKOCK, D.D. First Edition.

[Recommended by the Bishops of Bath and Wells, Ely, Lincoln, Southwell, and Wakefield.]

AURICULAR CONFESSION—SACRIFICIAL TERMS AND VESTMENTS—ALTAR—REAL PRESENCE.—" When we open the Communion Office [in the Second Prayer Book of Edward VI.] we are confronted with the same *reckless indifference to Catholic doctrine and practice*, and an ever-widening divergence from the lines laid down by the first Revisionists. . . . The concluding paragraph of the Exhortation, following the direction for such as were troubled in conscience to resort to the priest 'for comfort and absolution,' previously ran thus : ' requiring such as shall be satisfied with a General Confession, *not to be offended with them that do use, to their further satisfying, the Auricular and Secret Confession to the priest*, nor those also which think needful or convenient, for the quietness of their own consciences, particularly to open their sins to the priest, to be offended with them that are satisfied with their humble Confession to God, and the General Confession to the Church . . .' Few persons, who recognise the real teaching of the Church upon Confession and Absolution, *can fail to regret that such valuable counsel should have been removed* . . .

" In this revised Service, the Sacrificial aspect was greatly obscured by that of Communion. Sacrificial terms were for the most part suppressed ; sacerdotal vestments forbidden ; the position of the altar was changed, and the arrangement of important parts of the service disturbed. Everything, in short, was done, as the Revisionists fondly hoped, to dissociate the mind of the worshipper from all thoughts of oblation and sacrifice. . . . The term ' Altar,' which was the correlative of sacrifice, was erased from this and every other rubric, and Table or Holy Table substituted. The most honourable place occupied by the Altar all through the Church's history was left vacant, and the Table brought down to the body of the Church . . .

"In almost every Primitive Liturgy there had been a distinct prayer that the Spirit of God would sanctify the Elements that they might become to those who received them the Blessed Body and Blood of Christ. *To eliminate this then was to break away from Catholic usage* as well as to ignore the immediate action of the Holy Ghost. . . .

"Now the above is *a long and heavy bill of indictment* against the Second Revisionists *for departure from Catholic doctrine*" (pp. 91, 95, 96, 100-103, 106).

AN EXPLANATION OF THE THIRTY-NINE ARTICLES. By A. P. FORBES, D.C.L., Bishop of Brechin. Second Edition.

[Recommended by the Bishop of Lincoln.]

CHURCHES OF ROME AND THE EAST.—"Since no doctrine formerly received by all the Orthodox Eastern Patriarchates can be pointed out, which the Church of England can be held to have had in view when it declared [in Article XIX.] that these Patriarchates had erred, then neither, by the force of the terms, is any doctrine formerly received of the Latin Church intended, when it says that the Church of Rome had erred " (p. 272).

PURGATORY.—" We must come to the conviction that it was not the formulized doctrine, but a current and corrupt practice in the Latin or Western Church, which is here [Article XXII. 'Of Purgatory'] declared to be 'fond' and 'vainly invented'" (p. 303).

INTERCESSION OF SAINTS.—"If the intercession of believers on earth may be invoked, without injury to the honour of Christ as Mediator, why not also the intercession of the saints in heaven? Had this been all, the Article [XXII. on Invocation of Saints] never could have been written " (p. 423).

SEVEN SACRAMENTS.—" The septenary number of the Sacraments had long been held both by the Greek and Latin Churches, and there is no ground to deprive of a sacramental character the rites for which that character is claimed " (p. 448).

EXTREME UNCTION.—" The Unction of the Sick is the lost pleiad of the Anglican firmament. One must at once confess and deplore that a distinctly Scriptural practice has ceased to be commanded in the Church of England" (p. 465).

TRANSUBSTANTIATION.—" If 'substance' means no more than its Greek equivalent, οὐσία, 'essence'; and if the term ' is Transubstantiated' means no more than those old words 'becomes' 'is'; and if, by it, the Roman Church only means to guard with greater accuracy our Blessed Lord's words, 'This is My Body,' not contradicting anything which we know by experience. . . . There is nothing in such a statement which our Article [XXVIII.] denies, or which could form difficulty to any soul, which believed the blessed Presence of our Saviour, of His Body and his Blood " (p. 558).*

"THE SACRIFICE OF THE EUCHARIST."—"The Sacrifice in the Eucharist is substantially the same as the Sacrifice of the Cross, because the Priest is the same in both, and the Victim is the same in both " (p. 609).

AN INTRODUCTION TO THE HISTORY OF THE CHURCH OF ENGLAND. By HENRY O. WAKEMAN. Fifth Edition.

[Recommended by the Archbishop of York, and the Bishops of Bath and Wells, Ely, Oxford, Rochester, St. Albans, Wakefield, and Winchester.]

THE ENGLISH PROTESTANT MARTYRS.—" The vast majority of those [Protestants] who suffered [in Queen Mary's reign] were not people even of religious influence. They were illiterate *fanatics*" (p. 305).

EVANGELICAL CHURCHMEN.—" They interpreted the Prayer Book by the light of their own prepossessions. They cared little for its history and tradition, *ignored much of its teaching and ritual*, and valued it chiefly for the devotional beauty of its language " (p. 451).

TRACT XC.—" Newman argued [in Tract XC.] that there was no Catholic doctrine, and hardly any theological Roman doctrine, condemned by the Articles ; but only popular exaggerations and misrepresentations of Roman doctrine current at the time when the Articles were drawn up. Most men would now admit that, for the purpose which he had in hand, *Newman's argument was in the main sound* " (p. 475).

EUCHARISTIC VESTMENTS.†—" In the twenty years which followed the secession of Newman, prominent High Churchmen in all parts of the country began to restore the use of the Eucharistic Vestments and in other respects adopt the ceremonial which they believed to be authorised by the Ornaments Rubric. *Unfortunately the Bishops*, who for the most part had been brought up under Evangelical or Latitudinarian influences, *were unable to understand and sympathise with the real objects of this action* " (p. 483).

---

* The writer of this book (Bp. Forbes) had been formally censured after trial by the Scottish Bishops, and the above passage on Transubstantiation was framed by Dr. Pusey in consultation with "Cardinal" Newman *after* the latter had gone over to Rome. (Liddon's *Life of Pusey*, Vol. IV., p. 116.)

† The "Eucharistic Vestments" include the Popish Chasuble, Albe, Stole, Girdle, &c., all of which have been declared illegal by the Courts of Law.

THE "REAL" PRESENCE AND EUCHARISTIC SACRIFICE.—" Yet whatever difficulties and controversies the future may have in store, it can hardly again be questioned that the doctrines of the " Real " Presence and the Eucharistic Sacrifice have a legitimate place in the theology, worship, and devotional life of the Church of England " (p. 486).

THE OXFORD MOVEMENT—CONVENTS—PROTESTANTISM.—" The question therefore naturally arises, What is the special gift which it [the Oxford Movement] has brought to English religious life? what is the real secret of its power? Each revival of religion in the Church brings into fuller recognition *some special side of the mind of God*. What is it of *His purpose* which the Oxford Movement in its full development has made its own? . . It offered to the devout and spiritual a special vocation of obedience, of self-discipline, of retirement, of service, *in the consecrated life of the Cloister*. . . No man has become the weaker for submitting himself to the Oxford Movement. *There are many whose moral failure dates from their renunciation of it*. From the point of view of history the Church revival of the present century is seen to be nothing more than *the complete reaction against the Protestant Movement of the sixteenth century* " (pp. 490, 492).

WHAT THE OXFORD MOVEMENT MEANS.—" It means *the restoration of the Church of England to the position which it held when Edward VI. came to the throne*.* It means the repudiation of the teaching and the systems of Zwingli, Luther, and Calvin " (p. 493).

THE DOCTRINE OF THE PRIESTHOOD. By T. T. CARTER, M.A.
Second Edition.

[Recommended by the Bishop of Lincoln.]

SACRIFICE FOR THE LIVING AND THE DEAD.—" This Oblation, moreover, is made for the same ends and purposes for which our Lord offered Himself. And as He offered Himself for all for whom He was about to die,—not for the living only, but for those also who had gone before, and those who were to come afterwards—so our Sacrifice is offered, not merely for those present, or for those only who are alive on earth, but for those also who have ' died in the faith ' " (p. 40).

---

* That is, a restoration to the state of things which existed on the death of Henry VIII., for Mr. Wakeman censures severely the change which took place " on the accession of Edward VI." He declares that " the change was an unfortunate one for themselves and for England, *and especially unfortunate for the English Church*." The " position " of the English Church, on the accession of Edward VI. and before any change was made, was that of accepting almost every doctrine of Popery, excepting the Pope's Supremacy. The bloody Act of the " Six Articles " remained in force for more than twelve months after Henry's death.

CHURCH DOCTRINE, BIBLE TRUTH. By the Rev. M. F. SADLER.
Seventh Edition.

[Recommended by the Bishops of Chichester, Lincoln, Truro, and St. Albans.]

PRIESTLY MEDIATORSHIP. —" Does God bestow all things pertaining to salvation *directly from Himself*, or does God lead us to expect certain great blessings pertaining to salvation, *not directly, but indirectly*—through means of grace which He has Himself established, and of which means He ordains certain of our fellow-creatures to be the administrators? . . . It cannot be contrary to the glory of God that He should make use of subordinate agents and *outward visible signs to convey* even such things as cleansing and forgiveness " (pp. 218, 219).

" It is quite clear, then, that Christ set apart certain persons to be His Ministers, and put them into a remarkable position betwixt Himself and the rest of His followers " (p. 231).

A SACERDOTAL PRIESTHOOD.—" When, then, the Church was founded, the Saviour Himself appointed certain men to exercise *functions of a far more sacerdotal character* than ever exercised before, because the exercise of these functions was far more intimately connected with His own Atoning Sacrifice " (p. 235).

" It is clear, then, that not only were there ministers delegated by Christ Himself *to exercise the highest sacerdotal functions*, but also that provision was made that the exercise of those functions should be perpetual " (p. 238).

THE EVANGELICAL SYSTEM.—" I might have set forth *a large amount* of Scripture language, which those who adhere to the Evangelical system *eschew altogether*" (p. 382).

FAITH AND SALVATION.—" The Apostles do not teach that a man is saved as soon as he believes, even though he exercises the most lively act of faith " (p. 388).

THE ARIANS OF THE FOURTH CENTURY. By JOHN HENRY CARDINAL NEWMAN. Seventh Edition.

[Recommended by the Bishop of Lincoln.]

TRUTHFULNESS AND LYING.—" The Alexandrian Father who has already been quoted, *accurately* describes the rules which should guide the Christian in speaking and acting economically. ' Being fully persuaded of the omnipresence of God,' says Clement, ' and ashamed to come short of the truth, he is satisfied with the approval of God, and of his own conscience. Whatever is in his mind, is also on his tongue ; towards those who are fit recipients, both in speaking and living, he harmonises his profession with his thoughts. He both thinks and speaks the truth, *except when careful treatment is necessary*, and then, as a physician for the good of his patients, *he will lie, or rather utter a lie*, as the Sophists say " (p. 73).

AFTER DEATH. By H. M. LUCKOCK, D.D. First Edition.

[Recommended by the Bishop of Lincoln.]

INVOCATION OF SAINTS.—" Maintaining then as we do so great a regard for antiquity, we find it impossible to sympathise with those who desire to introduce Invocation [of Saints] into the forms of public worship. There can be little question that the Invocation, which the twenty-second Article describes 'as a vain thing fondly invented' [*N.B.* In a side-note to this passage Dr. Luckock writes thus: 'Article XXII. not condemnatory of every kind of Intercession'], was that form which was accompanied with worship; it is argued, therefore, that a prayer addressed to them without worship is permissible. Much, no doubt, may be said in favour of 'oblique prayer' or 'pious apostrophes of the dead'; *in themselves they may be not only harmless, but actually beneficial*; men's faith in the Communion of the Saints may be quickened thereby, *and their religious fervour increased*; but Catholic antiquity offers no support to their use, and the great Anglican divines show no signs in their writings of having adopted them " (pp. 256, 257).

PRAYERS FOR THE DEAD.—"The restoration of the primitive usage [of Prayers for the Dead] to its proper place in the Prayer Book, though surrounded with difficulties, which past experience forbids us to ignore, is yet an object to which men may look forward hopefully, and while striving to attain to it have no misgivings that they are acting in a spirit of true loyalty to the Church " (pp. 252, 253).

THE CHURCH TEACHERS' MANUAL. By the Rev. M. F. SADLER.
Thirteenth Thousand.

[Recommended by the Bishops of Chichester, Lichfield, and Lincoln.]

THE REAL PRESENCE.—"Is the Presence only in the heart of the receiver? No " (p. 321).

"Is it necessary that we should understand how, when we receive the Bread and Wine, we receive Christ's Body and Blood? No " (p. 327).

"The Apostle evidently makes the communion to depend upon the outward action (the blessing and breaking), in which the Bishop or Priest performs the act which Christ enjoined " (p. 325).

THE EUCHARISTIC SACRIFICE.—"The Church of Christ has *always* held it [the 'Holy Eucharist'] to be a sacrifice " (p. 308).

"Does the Sacrifice of praise and thanksgiving consist in the Hymns and words of praise and thanksgiving which are in the office? No " (p. 311).

FORGIVENESS OF SINS.—" What great privilege belongs to the Catholic Church The forgiveness of sins " (p. 156).

CONFESSION AND ABSOLUTION.—" Is it well that we should ever confess to a minister of the Church? At times it is " (p. 152).

" A minister of Christ being one whose business is the saving and oversight of souls, is most likely to guide us aright; and, secondly, the ministers of Christ are the commissioned ministers of reconciliation, who have the power of absolution committed to them. On both these grounds they are the natural recipients of such confessions as the Church encourages " (p. 153).

PRAYERS FOR THE DEAD.—" What fellowship in prayer have we? [with ' departed Saints ']. They pray for us. We pray for their rest, and the perfecting of their bliss " (p. 145).

SYMBOLISM. By J. A. MOEHLER, D.D.

[Recommended by the Bishop of Lincoln.]

This is a Roman Catholic attack on Protestantism which the translator describes as " a necessary supplement to Bossuet's *History of the Variations of the Protestant Churches.*"

THE WAFER IS THE TRUE CHRIST.—" The incarnate Son of God, who hath suffered, died and risen again from the dead for our sins, living, according to his own teaching, is present in the Eucharist, the Church from the beginning hath, at his command (Luke xxii.-20) substituted the Christ mystically present, and visible only to the spiritual eye of faith, for the historical Christ, now inaccessible to the bodily senses. The former is taken for the latter, because the latter is likewise the former—both are considered as one and the same: and the *Eucharistic Saviour*, therefore, as the victim also for the sins of the world " (I.-337). " With the Mass, accordingly, the faithful join the prayer, that *the merits of Christ*, which are considered as *concentrated in the Eucharistic sacrifice*, should be applied to all needing them and susceptible of them " (p. 342). " It is one and the same undivided victim—one and the same High Priest, who on the mount of Calvary *and* on our altars hath offered himself up an atonement for the sins of the world " (p. 346).

" This ordinance of Divine compassion necessarily leads, along with others, to the doctrine of *Internal Justification*: just as on the other hand *the Mass must be rejected with a sort of instinct wherever that doctrine is repudiated* " (p. 317).

Justification by faith is accordingly rejected, and Purgatory advocated, in this guide-book for Lincoln priestlings.

Some items of interest in connection with the conspiracy to Romanize the Church of England.

THE ASSOCIATION FOR PROMOTING UNITY OF CHRISTENDOM was founded by members of the Anglican, Greek, and Roman Churches, who are pledged to pray for "corporate re-union." The members' names are never published.

THE ORDER OF CORPORATE RE-UNION is a strictly secret organization. It is governed by "Bishops" (who are clergymen of the Church of England), deriving their "Orders" from some unknown source, **who secretly re-ordain other clergymen** of the Church of England while yet retaining their benefices within the Established Church. Of the three clergymen thus **secretly ordained** (on the high seas) *see* Brinckman's *Controversial Methods*, p. xvi], one was the Rev. T. W. Mossman, Rector of West Torrington, Lincolnshire, who before his death was received into the Church of Rome. The second is said to be the **Rev. Dr. Lee**, of All Saints', Lambeth, and the third is supposed to have been the late Rev. G. W. Nugee. All three having been members of the E. C. U. *The Whitehall Review*, however, quoted in *The Church Times* for March 14th, 1879, gives the following version:—"The three Anglican clerics who have obtained episcopal consecration from the Dutch Jansenists, for the purpose of 'revalidating' the Orders of clergymen having doubts about their priesthood, are singularly modest in their signatures. The 'Rector Provincial, Canterbury,' is '+ Thomas.,' the 'Provincial of Caerleon' is '+ Lawrence.,' the 'Provincial of York' is '+ Joseph.' Might I suggest that Bishop 'Thomas' sign for the future '+ Frederick George Lee;' Bishop 'Lawrence' '+ Joseph Leycester Lyne;' and Bishop 'Joseph' ' + Thomas W. Mossman'! Perhaps Bishop 'Lawrence' might prefer to call himself, ' + Ignatius;' if so, one would not object, as it would give a better idea of his real name." This statement has never been denied. The "Order" prays for the Pope as their Patriarch. The official organ of the E. C. U., *The Reunion Magazine*, p. 242, says: "We frankly acknowledge that, in the Providence of God, **the Roman Pontiff is the first Bishop in the Church,** and, therefore, its visible head on earth. . . . As the Church must have some executive head, and as there is no other competitor, we believe the Pope to be that head. But he is more to us than this, for he is our Patriarch as well."

THE SOCIETY OF ST. OSMUND.—The avowed "Intention" of this Society was to restore the Sarum Ritual and Use to the Reformed Church of England. It privately printed for the use of its members "The Services of Holy Week from the Sarum Missal," containing one for the idolatrous Veneration of the Cross, and an approval of the use of "Relics" and "Holy Water." This Society even went further, praying for the Pope as its "Father" and "blessed Pontiff." The list of Vice-Presidents contained the names of three Bishops, and that of Mr. Athelstan Riley, late of the London School Board. The Society has now been reorganised as "**the Alcuin Club,**" with the same Secretary and some of the same members of Committee, and with the **Bishops of Oxford, Salisbury, and Edinburgh** as members of the Club. Its present teaching is exposed in *The Church Intelligencer* for February, 1898.

THE GUILD OF ALL SOULS has for its object the offering of **Prayers for the Dead**, and **Masses to get souls out of Purgatory.** Nearly five hundred clergymen belong to this Guild. It has published *The Office of the Dead according to Roman and Sarum Uses.* The annual report of the Guild for 1892 states that "Requiem Celebrations" for the Dead are now offered, in connection with the Guild, in no fewer than 328 churches every month.

THE COWLEY "FATHERS" (Society of St. John the Evangelist, Cowley) at one time were members of the secret Society of the Holy Cross. They are all bound by perpetual **vows of poverty, chastity, and obedience.** At St. Alban's, Holborn, "Father Maturin" said: "I am Irish, I love Ireland, and all things Celtic, and, as a consequence, all things Roman" (*Church Times*, June 26th, 1896). In their pamphlet entitled *Suggestions for the Conduct of a Mission*, we read: "The clergy must be prepared to hear confessions at all times during a Mission, from morning to night. *Illiterate people will always require the help of the priest to question them*" (p. 7). The names of the 281 members are printed in the *C. A. Tract*, No. 246. Price 1d.

THE "HAIL, MARY".—At a meeting of the E. C. U. held in June, 1896, the Bishop of Nassau expressed his desire to get back the "Hail, Mary," and a " form for anointing the sick."

IMAGES of " the Virgin and Child " are now set up at **St. Paul's Cathedral, Westminster Abbey,** and **Kensington Parish Church.**

CONFESSION.—" Father " Black of the Cowley Brotherhood, an extreme Ritualist, in a sermon preached at St. Columba's, Kingsland Road, on April 23rd, 1896, said that, from **1200 to 1500 Clergy** of the Church of England are in the habit of hearing confession.

UNION WITH ROME.—On Thursday, March 21st, 1895, the **Pope gave audience to Lord Halifax** and Mr. J. W. Birkbeck, when the subject of Christian Unity was discussed. On Sunday, March 24th, the above gentlemen dined with Dr. Vaughan at the English College in Rome. Lord Halifax also assisted at a Mass celebrated by Dr. Vaughan. Yet we are constantly told that the English Church Union is " not a Romanizing Society."

The Lincoln Case.

A Judgment Four Times Revised since its Delivery. The Lambeth Judgment in the Bishop of Lincoln's case was remarkable for the unprecedented number of misquotations, sham vouchers, and misstatements of fact which it contained. That one Judgment alone embodied more grave blunders than have ever been alleged against the Privy Council decisions all put together, even if we could assume those charges to have been proved. But what is still more remarkable is the fact that since it was delivered a number of alterations have been secretly inserted! The first change was the substitution of "last revision" for "the Savoy Conference," intended to hide the Bishops' mistake in having attributed the revision of the Prayer Book to the abortive Savoy Conference. Next a list of seventeen corrections, some of them very material, was sent in by Sir John Hassard, the registrar of the Archbishop's Court, all of which are printed in *The Church Intelligencer* for October, 1893. Another alteration is found in the list published by Mr. Roscoe, the law reporter, which may be procured from Messrs. Clowes, the publishers.

In 1894 a second edition was published by Macmillan's, containing a list of "corrigenda" which *omits* two of the former corrections, which had been authorised and published by Archbishop Benson, yet it retains the unnoticed alteration first described, without *any* acknowledgment or any voucher. Lastly, on Appeal, the Privy Council three times over sanctioned the minister standing at that part of the table "which faces EASTWARD." Those words were repeated three times by the Lord Chancellor in open court, and were so printed in the official copies given out in court, as well as in the Reports of *The Times*, *Guardian*, and other papers, and in Dr. Cutts' *Handy Book of the Church of England*, published by the S. P. C. K.: yet this final Judgment of the Supreme Court has been stealthily reversed by changing "eastward" into "westward" (!) at some unknown period, and by some unknown authority. Litigation becomes worthless if published Judgments may be thus tampered with again and again: since in a few years' time the true text must become indiscoverable.

The Decisions in the Lambeth and Privy Council Judgments.

Eight points of ritual were charged against the Bishop of Lincoln and submitted to the courts for decision in this case. In the Court of the Archbishop at Lambeth, the Archbishop of Canterbury (Benson) declared the three following points to be illegal:—

1. Hiding the Manual Acts.
2. Making the sign of the cross.
3. Mixing the cup *during* the Service.

These points having been decided in accordance with the previous rulings by the Privy Council, no appeal was necessary. The decision of the Archbishop on the remaining five points, being considered unsatisfactory, an appeal was made to the Privy Council, and their Lordships decided as follows :—

4. Ministering a cup mixed *during* the Service. No decision was given on that point ; but if No. 3 is not done, No. 4 becomes impossible.
5. Lighted candles. No decision was given, as the Supreme Court held, that so far as this charge was concerned, the Bishop was not the person responsible. The previous decision of this Court, against burning lights " before the Sacrament " when not required for the purpose of giving light, therefore stands.
6. The charge was rinsing vessels and drinking the ablutions *during* the service. No decision as to the offence charged was given ; but the Court allowed the rinsing and drinking if done *after* the close of the Service. Drinking the ablutions *during* the Service, therefore, stands illegal, as by previous Judgments.
7. The Eastward Position during the Ante-Communion Service. This does not include the Prayer of Consecration. It was a new point raised for the first time, and was allowed by the Privy Council.
8. The singing of the " Agnus Dei." This was allowed by the Court.

Out of the eight points, therefore, raised in this case, No. 7, the Eastward Position in the Ante-Communion Service, and No. 8, the singing of the Agnus Dei, were the sole gains to the admirers of Mass Ritual.

The result put briefly is as follows :—

No. 1. Hiding the manual acts during the Prayer of Consecration . **Illegal**
No. 2. Making the sign of the cross . **Illegal**
No. 3. Mixing the cup *during* the Service . . **Illegal**
No. 4. Administering a cup mixed *during* the Service. No decision, but the ruling in No. 3 renders it . **Illegal**
No. 5. Lighted Candles. No decision : but by previous Judgments . **Illegal**
No. 6. Rinsing vessels and drinking the wine and water used for their "ablutions" *during* the Service. No decision : but by previous decisions . **Illegal**
No. 7. Eastward Position in Ante-Communion Service . *Legal*
No. 8. The " Agnus Dei " *Legal*

It has been suggested that the Bishops have no power; but the following shews some action which may be taken by any Diocesan Bishop:—

(i) May exclude from Ordination those who refuse to pledge themselves to conform to the law.

(ii) May refuse to license curates to any law-breaking incumbent, and inhibit all others from giving him assistance.

(iii) May withdraw the licences of curates who assist in illegal acts.

(iv) May issue monitions to lawless clergy which can be enforced by ecclesiastical punishments.

(v) May refuse to consecrate places of worship where illegal ornaments are introduced.

(vi) May himself take proceedings under the Church Discipline Act.

(vii) May facilitate proceedings of aggrieved parishioners, and refuse to shelter lawless acts by a wanton abuse of the statutory Veto.

(viii) May refuse to hold Confirmations in churches where the law is broken.

(ix) May refuse to institute to a benefice a clergyman who has been in the habit of breaking the law, and who declines to promise not to repeat the illegal acts. All such matters as would be good causes for deprivation are grounds of refusal to institute. (*Heywood* v. *Bp. of Manchester*, 12 Q. B. D., 404.)

(x) May order the removal from a church all illegal ornaments introduced without a Faculty.

(xi) May forbid the clergy of his diocese to use any service not found in the Book of Common Prayer.

(xii) May refuse to sanction by his presence any act or ceremony which has been declared illegal by the Queen's Courts.

(xiii) May inhibit law-breaking clergy, not under his jurisdiction, from officiating or preaching in his diocese.

(xiv) May inhibit law-breaking clergy, under his jurisdiction, from officiating or preaching outside their parishes, in other churches in his diocese.

Statistics shewing to some extent how the Church

	Canterbury	York	London	Winchester	Durham	Bangor	Bath & Wells	Bristol	Carlisle	Chester	Chichester	Ely	Exeter	Gloucester
1. No. of Ritualistic Incumbents	208	188	373	252	112	19	126	62	45	94	155	192	173	116
2. No. of Ritualistic Curates	152	118	625	196	138	22	70	63	29	87	132	90	123	59
3. Total number of Ritualistic Clergy in Diocese	360	306	998	448	250	41	196	125	74	181	287	282	296	175
4. No. of Churches and Mission-churches served by the above Clergy	242	215	386	280	125	25	131	65	48	105	174	221	196	136
5. No. of Parishes, served by the above Incumbents, in which there is no other Church for Protestants to attend	105	127	20	151	55	15	89	29	26	53	88	139	106	78
6. No. of Parishes in which the Church Day Schools under the above pernicious influence are the only Schools for the children of Protestant Churchmen and Dissenters to attend	113	107	19	141	50	13	77	36	23	65	77	102	83	77
7. No. of Parishes in which Romish Vestments are illegally worn	33	64	95	13	22	1	45	21	3	16	31	60	50	32
8. No. of Parishes in which Incense is illegally used	7	18	45	18	2	1	14	6	1	6	19	11	19	13
9. No. of Parishes in which "Altar" Lights are illegally burnt	121	128	206	158	52	3	86	40	18	50	91	149	133	87
10. No. of Parishes in which the mixed Chalice is illegally used	93	100	164	127	65	2	76	31	20	49	88	131	117	73
11. No. of Parishes in which the Manual Acts are illegally hid	197	182	286	258	103	15	117	59	42	93	148	186	172	119

The authority for most of the above statistics is *The Tourists' Church Guide*. The authority for the statistics as to " Church Day Schools " is Education The extent to which the *present* Bishops are responsible for the appointment We would draw special attention to the grievance of Protestant Churchmen

of England is being Romanized in each Diocese.

Hereford	Lichfield	Lincoln	Liverpool	Llandaff	Manchester	Newcastle	Norwich	Oxford	Peterborough	Ripon	Rochester	St. Albans	St. Asaph	St. David's	Salisbury	Sodor & Man	Southwell	Truro	Wakefield	Worcester
83	215	162	70	68	162	76	158	280	233	97	202	255	30	40	199	5	162	155	63	170
30	173	87	87	110	145	64	72	147	110	84	295	181	36	29	103	2	94	66	64	135
113	388	249	157	178	307	140	230	427	343	181	497	436	66	69	302	7	256	221	127	305
92	233	180	72	81	179	97	173	320	255	110	230	286	31	49	216	6	186	182	71	190
60	28	108	21	37	58	42	105	186	169	53	35	161	19	26	141	2	96	118	37	84
62	138	104	26	35	66	44	84	184	144	43	45	162	20	30	161	3	94	65	38	88
17	45	67	13	27	17	24	49	178	35	16	46	54	4	5	34	2	59	47	19	37
4	8	13	5	7	4	11	15	18	8	7	14	19	—		6	1	13	4	9	11
60	110	126	22	47	51	46	112	204	133	67	122	170	10	24	124	2	110	119	38	101
37	114	93	29	38	79	48	101	159	115	57	111	149	10	18	136	2	102	110	46	96
84	191	166	55	63	141	72	156	295	212	97	188	251	26	42	184	5	164	170	67	171

compiled and published by the English Church Union.
Dept. Blue Book, c.-8546.
of the above Incumbents has been shewn in the previous pages
under No. 5, and of Protestant Churchmen and Dissenters under No. 6.

Of the Bishops herein referred to the following were Appointed or Translated by Lord Salisbury:

See.	Consecrated.	Translated.	See page
Canterbury (Temple) ...	1869	1897	39
York (Maclagan) ...	1878	1891	44
London (Creighton) ...	1891	1897	48
Winchester (Davidson)	1890	1895	51
Durham (Westcott) ...	1890	—	53
Bangor (Lloyd)	1890		54
Bristol (Browne)	1895	1897	57
Carlisle (Bardsley)	1887	1892	
Chester (Jayne) ...	1889	—	58
Chichester (Wilberforce)	1882	1895	60
Ely (Compton)	1886	—	62
Lichfield (Legge) ...	1891		70
Manchester (Moorhouse)	1876	1886	77
Newcastle (Jacob)	1896	—	79
Oxford (Stubbs)	1884	1888	81
Peterborough (Glyn) ...	1897		84
Rochester (Talbot) ...	1895		86
Salisbury (Wordsworth)	1885		88
St. Albans (Festing) ...	1890		93
St. Asaph (Edwards) ...	1889		96
St. Davids (Owen ...	1897		
Sodor and Man (Stratton)	1892		
Truro (Gott) ...	1891		97
Wakefield (Eden) ...	1890	1897	99
Worcester (Perowne) ...	1891		

By Mr. Gladstone:

Exeter (Bickersteth) ...	1885	64
Lincoln (King) ...	1885	72
Llandaff (Lewis) ...	1883	75
Norwich (Sheepshanks)	1893	80
Ripon (Carpenter)	1884	85
Southwell (Ridding) ...	1884	90

By Lord Rosebery:

Bath and Wells (Kennion)	1882	1894	55
Hereford (Percival) ...	1895		69

By Lord Palmerston:

Gloucester (Ellicott) ...	1863	66

By Lord Beaconsfield:

Liverpool (Ryle)	1880

STATISTICAL ABSTRACT SHEWING THE GROWTH OF ROMISH PRACTICES IN THE CHURCH OF ENGLAND AT HOME AND ABROAD.

PARTICULARS.	1882	1883	1884	1885	1886	1888	1890	1892	1894	1896	1898
Churches	2,581	2,795	3,319	3,426	3,476	3,776	4,455	5,042	5,957	7,062	8,183
Daily Holy Eucharist	123	143	147	157	156	200	253	306	406	474	613
Eucharistic Vestments	336	359	396	449	509	589	797	1,029	1,370	1,632	2,026
Incense	9	16	22	38	66	89	135	177	250	307	381
Altar Lights at the Holy Eucharist	581	663	749	869	968	1,136	1,402	2,048	2,707	3,568	4,334
Mixed Chalice										2,111	4,030
Eastward Position	1,662	1,876	2,054	2,258	2,433	2,690	3,138	3,918	5,037	5,964	7,044
Free	1,098	1,194	1,312	1,416	1,559	1,744	2,070	2,454	3,135	3,263	3,767
Open for Private Prayer	1,121	1,222	1,332	1,463	1,634	1,841	2,230	2,744	3,382	3,648	4,282

The above statistics are taken from *The Tourists' Church Guide*, compiled and published by the English Church Union.

www.ingramcontent.com/pod-product-compliance
Lightning Source LLC
Chambersburg PA
CBHW020130170426
43199CB00010B/710